THE SECOND WORLD WAR

PART 3
The Motorised Armies, Scandinavia,
Italy and the Axis Satellites,
the Navy and Naval Air Arms,
the United States, Japan and China

Liliane and Fred Funcken

Prentice-Hall, Inc., Englewood Cliffs, N.J.

Contents

Foreword

With this, the third and penultimate volume on the Second World War, we survey the uniforms of a number of countries, such as Norway, Finland, Bohemia, Slovakia and Croatia, many of which will be unfamiliar to the reader.

Along with Italy and the Fascist militia of Mussolini, this volume also covers the forces of the United States and of their great enemies, the Japanese.

Once again, it has not been possible to follow strict chronological order for those reasons already given in the foreword to part one of this series. It is in this volume, therefore, that we first come to the sea battles, during which the Royal Navy proved that it had lost nothing of its force or courage as a naval power. The French fleet too, the traditional allies, is also included, together with the small Belgian navy whose survivors served proudly under their own country's colours in the heart of the British battle fleet.

We would like to offer our sincere thanks to the following people for their invaluable help:
Colonel E. Grimaldi, Curator of the Italian Cavalry Museum at Pinerolo,
Lieutenant Brynhildsen of the Army Museum at Oslo,
Lieutenant-Colonel Palmen and the Curator of the Finnish Armed Forces' Historical Institute.

PART ONE
THE MOTORISED ARMIES

Tanks and self-propelled guns played a fundamentally important role from the earliest months of the Second World War, as has been outlined in volume 2. But alongside these there was a great army of vehicles which were, perhaps, less spectacular, but which were vital to mobilise the armed forces.

At the outbreak of hostilities Germany introduced an impressive array of troop carriers in which the tracked vehicle held an important place. This rumbling armada swept all over Europe, seeing action all the way; but, bit by bit, it was eaten away by wear and tear and by the increasingly heavy blows inflicted by the enemy, and it was eventually to be swamped by the formidable industrial power of the Allies.

To illustrate even one-tenth of the utility vehicles which were put into service by the major fighting powers would have taken up the whole of a book of this kind. We have therefore deliberately limited their representation in this volume to a few machines, but examples of other interesting types will feature in the fourth and final volume, particularly in the chapters on Russia, America and Japan.

play a very important part in the war, which was becoming more of a certainty as each day went by. No one had forgotten that twenty years earlier mechanisation had made possible the great offensive of 1918, in which Marshal Foch had struck repeated blows at the enemy. It was also recalled how much the lack of tracked artillery pieces had been felt during the strategic retreat ordered by Hindenburg who, by dynamiting a few roads, had won his troops a breathing-space of forty-eight hours.

Speed and the ability to cross rough terrain were therefore considered as the two main problems to be solved. Two opposing technical solutions were very soon put forward and both the six-wheeled vehicle and the tracked vehicle each had their own supporters.

In the case of the tracked vehicle it was quickly recognised that it was likely to cause damage to the roads, but Citroën produced a light track known as the 'Kégresse-Hinstin', which was quiet and flexible and ingeniously combined steel and rubber in its construction.

The 'six-wheelers' produced by several manufacturers, of which the most famous was Laffly,

France

FRANCE AND THE ARMY ON WHEELS

The French military authorities were not slow to recognise that the motor vehicle was likely to

L. & F. FUNCKEN

actually used five pairs of wheels, but two pairs were merely auxiliaries and were only called into play when they came into contact with the ground as the vehicle was crossing slopes or ridges. The main wheels could actually be lowered individually so that they moulded themselves independently to the obstacle in question, thanks to the remarkable arrangement of the universal joint. However, the great disadvantage of the six-wheelers was their tendency to get bogged down in mud or deep snow, while the tracked vehicle could cross practically any type of surface thanks to its much larger area of contact with the ground and the wider distribution of its weight. However, the adoption of low-pressure pneumatic tyres (28.2 oz) and very strong mouldings greatly improved the performance of the six-wheelers and their superior speed, together with lower fuel consumption, helped them to compete with the tracked vehicles on an equal footing.

The problem of crossing water-courses, in short of finding or providing adequate bridges which, in some ten thousand cases, would not have supported a lorry of more than five tons, was indeed very tricky. It was therefore necessary to equip mechanised units with bridging devices capable of guaranteeing their role as the rapid and mobile elements of the army. Because it was short of such equipment, the French armoured and motorised army of the period could be considered better adapted to the defensive rather than the offensive role.

These difficulties, which on the whole are overlooked by the layman, slowed down innumerable actions and caused delays and bottlenecks throughout the war. These delays had a profound influence on the course of various battles and, paradoxically, made armies the victims of their own intensive motorisation.

One other problem remained which was less immediately apparent but much more difficult to resolve: this lay in the industrial potential of the country and its capacity for mass production in wartime.

As early as 1936 France had begun to elaborate plans for a more rational organisation, though without copying Germany, that disturbing neighbour who had already re-equipped her army on a massive scale. In the hope of avoiding an unnecessary drain on public funds, the Ministry tried to promote the sale to the public of special vehicles which could be requisitioned by the army if war broke out. One suspects that this curious scheme met with little success.

Some small comfort could be gained by drawing up a list of the private vehicles, including lorries, coaches, buses, tractors and touring-cars, that might be available and which totalled 1,200,000 in 1936. Unfortunately, many of these vehicles would have been virtually useless because of the lack of maintenance that was largely due to the economic crisis which plagued the period.

Only one valuable step forward was achieved: the standardisation of towing attachments on specialised vehicles.

THE MILITARY TRANSPORT TRAIN [1] IN WARTIME

The transport train, which is to the army what blood and the circulatory system are to the body, had been somehow or other adapted to meet the situation in spite of its heterogeneous equipment. This indispensable corps was split into two, with motor vehicles on one side and horses and mules on the other. Notices indicated to convoys the motor roads or the routes to be taken by horse-

1 The element of an army which is responsible for road transport.

VARIOUS MILITARY VEHICLES

1. Latil light artillery tractor (France)—2. Brossel TAL heavy artillery tractor (Belgium)—3. FN Tricar motor-tricycle (Belgium). Although not widely distributed, several versions of this machine nevertheless existed—4. AEC Matador medium artillery tractor (Great Britain)—5. Fiat/Spa TM40 medium artillery tractor (Italy)

1

2

3

2F.Fundin

4

5

drawn vehicles, the latter sometimes following winding paths across fields.

Regiments had been replaced by companies of four sections; sometimes several companies together formed a group. A division, in theory, had two transport companies; an army corps had three, while an army had a variable number of transport and medical companies at its disposal, these being commanded by a headquarters staff.

The section was the smallest existing unit and the numbers of men and vehicles varied greatly from section to section. The transport section had twenty buses or twenty lorries, or twenty-five vans or even twenty-five touring cars for personnel and for equipment. All these vehicles were of the same type and mark. The highway section comprised twenty to twenty-five lorries or tractors, the medical section, twenty vehicles.

In addition there was a reserve at the disposal of the general headquarters, made up of several groups, each with a headquarters staff, one headquarters company, seven heavy companies, one company of light motor lorries or vans, and one light company, with a total strength of 14,000 men in each group.

To control this mass, the men of the traffic squads prepared and marked out routes, put up directional signs or accompanied convoys, even acting as police on the road. Riding motor-cycles or travelling in light vehicles, these soldiers on point duty at cross-roads could be recognised by their white batons and their green and white armbands (with the white stripe above the green), which they wore on the left arm.

In 1939 the zone of the armies was divided into sectors or connected to so many road control centres. Each sector had some thirty traffic squads at its disposal. It was further sub-divided into a number of districts from which those responsible would keep the central control point informed about the progress of the operations of each squad and about the movement of convoys. The convoys thus passed from the area supervised by one control point to another without ever ceasing to be under the vigilant care of these unassuming and often unappreciated auxiliaries.

Great Britain

Between the two World Wars Britain had been slow in coming to grips with the problem of motorisation but had eventually been able to resolve it in a more satisfactory fashion than France, given the fact that her armed forces were smaller. The Royal Army Service Corps, like the units of the Royal Engineers, no longer possessed a single horse-drawn vehicle. The artillery itself, which had previously needed some two hundred horses to move and support a six-gun battery, was henceforth moved about behind powerful tracked vehicles known as 'dragoons' which were four- to six-wheeled cross-country gun tractors.

After the disastrous Battle of France, some 5,000 vehicles of all types, which had earlier been landed on the Continent, were saved and taken back to Britain.[1]

The production of this type of equipment was immediately initiated on a massive scale and Great Britain, determined to fight to the bitter end, obtained an impressive array of vehicles of all kinds from the United States and Canada. By the end of the war, Britain had over 1,250,000 military vehicles in service.

1 As early as September 1939, 24,000 vehicles had landed in France.

Germany

Between 1932 and 1939 an extraordinary armada of highly specialised vehicles was assembled under the direction of the Nazi leaders who presided over German re-armament. Having become a rich field for engineers, Germany was provided with a mass of military vehicles with a level of technical perfection that no other country in the world would have dreamed of achieving. However, the cost of this re-armament was so phenomenally high and the actual results so poor that, in the event, these marvellous machines carried only a very small number of Germany's fighting men. On the other hand, their propaganda value was incalculable. A clear-thinking General, von Schnell, brought an end to this orgy of ingenuity and reduced the number of different models in production from 300 to 80, among which could be found the famous little 'Kübelwagen', or bucket-seated car, whose descendants, the Volkswagen 'Beetles', still fill the roads of the entire world. It is an astonishing but undeniable fact, however, that the horse-drawn vehicle retained an important place in the German forces.

Having been forced to abandon their unrealistic hopes of a rapid victory, the leaders of the Third Reich found themselves, as the months went by, increasingly incapable of providing the Wehrmacht with the equipment that it needed to keep the upper hand. The factories commandeered in the occupied countries were never sufficient in number or output to rectify this situation; the lack of raw materials and the frightful effects of the Allied bombing did the rest.

Italy

Having first engaged in hostilities as early as 1935, Fascist Italy had some excellent military transport vehicles well before 1940, which were being produced by the firms of Alfa-Romeo, Fiat, Lancia and others. In numbers, however, they never matched those possessed by the other major fighting nations.

Soviet Union

The first purely Soviet lorry made its appearance in 1924. By 1928 the USSR was producing 50,000 lorries a year and in 1937 70,000 were built by the firm of ZIS alone. A few months after the German attack of June 1941 the Soviet Union began to receive, for its transport units, the half-million American, Canadian or British vehicles that played a significant part in the formidable offensive which, from 1943 to 1945, took the Red army to Berlin itself.[1]

1 The principal Soviet vehicles will be shown in vol. 4.

GERMAN ARMY VEHICLES (pages 12–13)

1. Sd.Kfz.10 (Demag D7) 1-ton light half-track—2. Sd.Kfz.6 5-ton medium half-track—3. Sd.Kfz.9 (FAMO F2) 18-ton heavy half-track—4. Sd.Kfz.10/4 (Demag D7) half-track with the 2cm Flak 38 anti-aircraft gun—5. Kfz.70 Auto-Union/Horsch heavy cross-country reconnaissance or staff car—6. NSU 'Kettenrad' semi-truck motorcycle—7. Kfz.1 (Volkswagen Type 82) light car—8. Kfz.1/20 ('Schimmwagen') (Volkswagen Type 166) light amphibious car. 52,000 examples of the former and more than 14,000 examples of the latter were produced—9–11. Feldgendarmerie

PART TWO

SCANDINAVIA

The Norwegian Army

Never has a country presented such an unwarlike image as Norway. An examination of her uniforms alone provides evidence of an attitude that was fiercely neutral and pacifist. A system which combined compulsory service with militia units had long given Norway an army organised around six-brigade cadres, whose effective peacetime strength reached 8,000 men in winter and 10,000 in summer from a total population of about 3,000,000.

The war struck this peaceful nation like a thunderbolt with the simultaneous landings of German troops at six major ports spread over 1,000 miles of coastline, while Bergen, Kristiansand, Oslo and Stavanger were captured without a shot being fired by parachute and airborne troops. Coupled with the element of surprise, treason also contributed greatly towards the success of the *Weserübung*,[1] the pro-Nazi supporters of Vidkun Quisling having spared no efforts, even within the Norwegian Army and administration themselves, to facilitate a 'peaceful conquest'. Moreover, the soldiers of the Wehrmacht had received orders to carry out the occupation of Norway by the least brutal methods possible: they were only to use their weapons if they came under fire, but they should nevertheless smash all such resistance with the utmost vigour.

As nearly always happens in the case of a surprise attack, the victims reacted in a confused and unco-ordinated fashion. The mobilisation plan could not be put into effect and only a few units stationed outside the towns could be properly organised, while, in the north, the 6th Infantry Brigade constituted the only force of any

significance that was immediately available.

In other places, such as at Narvik, the Norwegian conscripts were so unprepared that they allowed General Dietl's forces to land without firing a shot, for fear that they might be shooting at British troops! The more prudent Germans had, in fact, just sunk the *Norge*, which had tried to oppose their landing.[2]

Around Oslo, where they had deployed powerful air and naval forces, the aggressors were held in check by a few gunners of the fortress of Oscarborg. With their old 280mm coast-defence guns and two well-aimed torpedoes, they neatly sank the cruiser *Blücher* and, with her, 800 sailors and 1,500 invasion troops; only 200 survivors were picked up.

---

1 See vol. 1, page 49.
2 See 'The Norwegian Navy' in the general chapter on the navies of various fighting powers.

NORWEGIAN ARMY I

Ranks: 1. Generalmajor (Major-General)—2. Oberst (Colonel)—3. Oberstloitnant (Lieutenant-Colonel)—4. Major—5. Kaptein (Captain)—6. Premierloitnant (Lieutenant)—7. Sekondloitnant (Second Lieutenant)—8. Officer Candidate—9. Kommandersersjant (Company Sergeant-Major)—10. Furer (Sergeant-Major)—11. Sersjant (Sergeant)—12. Korporal (Lance-Corporal)

13. Detail of kepi decoration—14. Lieutenant in field service dress, 1914 pattern—15. Lieutenant in 1934 pattern uniform (little worn)—16. 6.5mm carbine, 1912 model—17. 0.45 calibre Colt automatic pistol, Norwegian 1914 model—18. 6.5mm Krag-Jorgensen rifle, 1894 model

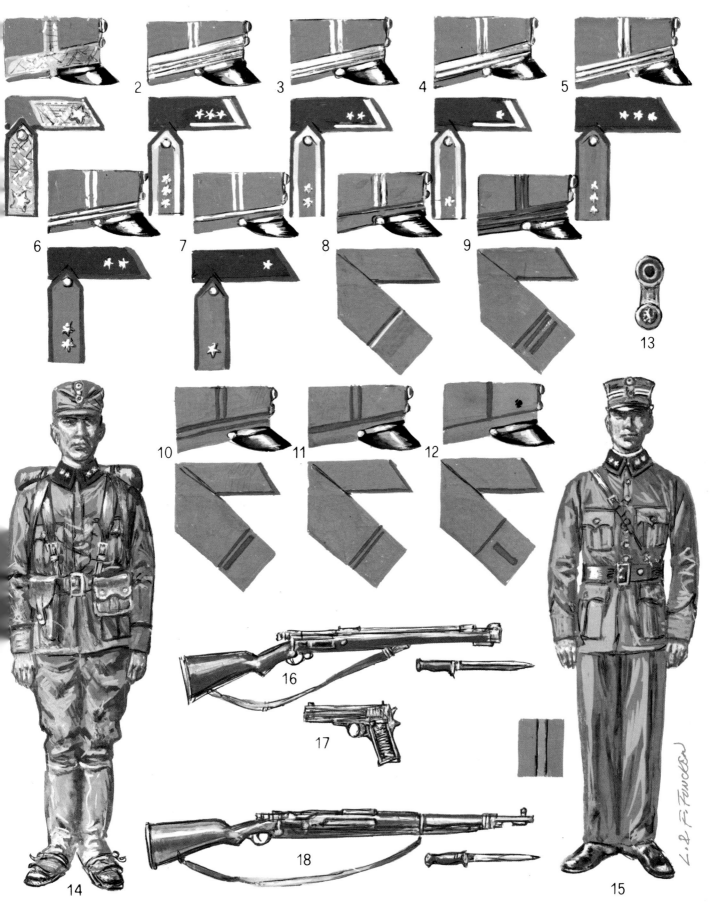

2

3

4

5

6

7

8

9

10

11

12

13

14

15

16

17

18

The more fortunate paratroops took possession of Fornebu aerodrome after a brief struggle. They made their entry the same afternoon into a subdued Oslo and 1,400 lightly armed troops paraded through the streets of the Norwegian capital under the frightened gaze of thousands of its inhabitants.

What could now be achieved by the stalwart Major-General Otto Ruge, who had been charged by the Norwegian government with the task of organising the resistance? First, he could respond to calls to capitulate with a few heartfelt words: 'We do not wish to surrender, for our struggle has only just begun'. Second, he could then persuade his slender forces to perform their soldierly duty by pushing back the invader. In the north one battalion stopped Dietl's forces, which had just come from Narvik after having forced the garrison there to surrender; in the centre of the country, the commander of the Vth military district pressed on with the mobilisation of his sector some way to the north of Trondheim. Further south, at Hegra, a resolute officer, one Major Heltermann, held the old fort with a few gunners, while in the central region at Gol, and in the south at Stavanger, brave officers gathered their men together.

All this time, however, German reinforcements had continued to flow in by air and sea and they now began the task of conquering Norway by the well-tried *Blitzkrieg* techniques. With air supremacy and with the main routes of land communication in their hands, the Germans gained a little more ground each day in their race against the Allies, who finally arrived too late to prevent the conquest of the entire country.[1] After two months of fighting, from 8 April to 7 June 1940, this conquest was completed, by a cruel irony, on the very day of the 35th Anniversary of Norwegian Independence. Too often passed over in silence, 1,335 Norwegian soldiers had given their lives in the defence of their country.

[1] See vol. 1, pages 49–50.

THE NORWEGIAN SOLDIER

It is the dated appearance of the Norwegian uniform that strikes one at first glance, although this is hardly surprising since, even in its latest form, it goes back to 1921 and, to a very large extent, to an even older pattern introduced in 1914. These two uniforms often found themselves combined on the same individual, in particular the 1921 pattern headdress and the 1914 pattern uniform. A third, more modern type introduced in 1934 differed mainly in the green colour of the piping, but it was much less widely worn.

The 1914 pattern kepi was the oldest element of the uniform, its distinctive shape and style being clearly seen in the illustrations. It was worn concurrently with the 1921 pattern kepi, which was plainly more practical and sober in appearance.

Two types of steel helmet also existed: one was the British 1916 pattern Mark I helmet, the other being a purely Norwegian model introduced into service in 1935. The latter, which was fairly deep with a slightly raised crown, looked somewhat like the old *cabasset* worn by arquebusiers. An oval plate (or plaque), which was decorated in relief with an heraldic lion wielding an axe, was brazed on the front of the helmet.

The trousers, worn outside and over the boots in normal weather, were tucked into high linen or webbing gaiters in winter to stop snow from getting into the boots.

NORWEGIAN ARMY II

1. Officer in fur-lined tunic—2. Airman with the special field service cap—3. Officer in the 1914 pattern uniform—4. Infantryman in the 1914 pattern uniform and the British 1916 pattern steel helmet—5. Cavalryman in the 1934 pattern uniform—6. Infantryman with the old 1914 pattern uniform and the *Jäger*-type peaked cap, without piping—7–8. Infantrymen in the 1934 pattern uniform and the 1935 pattern steel helmet

Airmen wore the uniform, or rather one of the uniforms, of the general pattern, but with the following distinguishing features:

1 A pair of spread wings, over a circle round the letter 'S', which surmounted a small crown on an heraldic button, the whole device being in silver.

2 A British-style field service (or side) cap was optional wear. The braid on the front was surmounted by the national cockade and finished with an heraldic button, similar to that which adorned the headdress of other arms of service.

WEAPONS

The rifle was the 6.5mm Krag-Jorgensen model 1894 and the machine-gun was the old water-cooled Colt.

The 75mm field gun and the 81mm howitzer constituted the main armament of the artillery.

THE AIR FORCE

The Norwegian air force was extremely weak, possessing only 9 Gloster Gladiator fighters and a few He.115 aircraft, all biplanes which could be described as reasonably modern. All the other machines, Fokkers and Tiger Moths, were hopelessly obsolete.

The fighter squadron consisted of 22 officers and NCOs and 92 men of other ranks. All responded to the call of duty with admirable courage but, on 9 April, the Norwegian fighter force lost practically all its aircraft. The airmen were then re-organised into a single squadron called 'Group R', which fought on in the north of the country until the very end. Several pilots escaped to Britain and distinguished themselves throughout the war in the ranks of the Royal Air Force.

The Finnish Army

Before Finland entered the war on 30 November 1939 no one cared very much about this 'small' country of 400,000 square kilometres, nor about her 3,800,000 or so inhabitants whose intellectual level was, however, particularly high.

It was thanks to her 150,000 soldiers, noted for their strong discipline founded on religious and patriotic inspiration, to her volunteers and civic guards, almost equal in number and, finally, to the 50,000 women of the Lotta League that Finland was to win the admiration of the whole world.

Finland's national consciousness had only begun to be awakened in the nineteenth century under the yoke of the Russian Czars, although this yoke was in fact relatively light, since Finland enjoyed a genuine measure of internal autonomy. This growing national awareness had been stimulated by the publication by Elias Lönnrot of the 22,000-verse *Kalevala*, a collection of epic songs dating back centuries. Thus the Finnish people were strongly opposed to the measures of 'Russianisation' that Nicholas II sought to impose on them during the closing years of the century.

FINNISH ARMY I

Ranks: 1. Marshal—2. General (infantry)—3. Lieutenant-General (artillery)—4. Brigadier-General (air force)—5. Colonel (staff)—6. Lieutenant-Colonel (reserve troops)—7. Major (signals)—8. Captain (rifles)—9. Lieutenant (engineers)—10. Second Lieutenant (tanks)—11. General (medical service)—12. Captain (veterinary branch)—13. Chaplain—14. Engineer Officer—15. Major (administrative branch)—16. Bandmaster—17. Detail of the heraldic lion denoting the senior ranks—18. Detail of the hawthorn-flower emblem denoting ranks below Brigadier-General—19. Company Sergeant-Major (artillery)—20. Sergeant-Major (coast artillery)—21. Sergeant (engineers)—22. Corporal (signals)—23. Lance-Corporal (infantry)—24. Trooper (cavalry)

25. Officer's field service cap—26. Cap worn by other ranks, with piping according to the colour of the arm of service—27. Field service tunic, 1927 pattern—28. Field service tunic, 1936 pattern—*Shoulder strap insignia:* 29. Engineers—30. Musicians—31. Administrative Branch—32. Signals—33. Pioneers—34. Infantry

The metal badges seen in figs 2–10 replaced the insignia on the raincoat and cloak.

1

2

5

8

3

6

9

4

7

10

11

12

13

14

15

17

16

18

20

21

22

23

24

25

26

27

29

30

31

32

33

34

28

L. & F. FUNCKEN

The collapse of Imperial Russia in 1917 was not synonymous with Finland's liberation. It led in fact to a confrontation between the activists of the right and the social-democrats of the extreme left, whose 'Red Guards' were supported by 40,000 Bolshevik soldiers.

The civil war broke out on 27 January 1918 and became a cruel and pitiless struggle between 'White' and 'Red' brothers who now found themselves to be enemies. The 'Whites' triumphed after two months of conflict. They owed their victory to the invaluable contribution of 2,000 Finnish soldiers who had been secretly trained in Germany, the *Jäger* (riflemen), and above all to the intervention of a German expeditionary force of 12,000 men placed under the command of General Rüdiger von der Goltz.

On 16 May 1918 Finland became free, at least in theory, since Germany proposed as her King the Kaiser's brother-in-law, Prince Frederick Charles of Hesse. The victory of the Allies frustrated this plan and it was General Carl Gustav Emil Mannerheim, the former commander of the 'White' forces, who was named Regent of the new State.

After becoming a republic in 1919, Finland was not judged as an ally of Germany by the Paris Peace Conference. A peace treaty was signed with Russia in 1920 and the new State slowly took shape, in spite of a serious linguistic conflict between the Swedish-speaking Finns of the *Svenska Folkpartet* (the Swedish Popular Party) and the Finnish-speaking section of the population.[1] Governments succeeded each other with increasing rapidity as a result of perpetual disputes between the right and the Communists, and the latter ended up by becoming victims of discriminatory measures. However, all this agitation did not prevent important reforms from being instituted, such as the agrarian law which made numerous poor farmers the owners of their own land.

Having decided to maintain a strictly neutral posture, Finland concluded a non-aggression pact with the USSR in 1932. However, the sky suddenly darkened in September 1939, when the Germano-Soviet Pact recognised Finland as coming within the Soviet sphere of influence. Summoned to Moscow the following month, a Finnish delegation found themselves faced with Soviet demands for 1) a rectification of the frontier in the Karelian Isthmus to a depth of ten kilometres; and 2) the lease of the land necessary for the establishment of a Soviet naval base on the Gulf of Finland, in the Hangö peninsula to the west of Helsinki. The Soviet Union would agree in turn to a significant territorial compensation (of 5,000 square kilometres) in Soviet Karelia and to the fortification by Finland of the Åland islands. In addition, the Russians would drop their demands relating to a mutual assistance pact, which the Finns found a little too military for their taste.

Very reluctantly Finland finally accepted these conditions with one exception: namely, the Soviet demand for a naval base, which was judged to threaten Finland's independence. The negotiations were broken off on 13 November after six weeks of discussions and on 28 November the USSR renounced the non-aggression pact of 1932. From that moment war became inevitable.

FINNISH ARMY II

1. 1927 pattern uniform. Note the pointed and turned-up toes of the boots—2–3. 1936 pattern uniform, front and back views—4. As above, with the Finnish steel helmet—5. Equipment introduced at the end of the war—6. Officers in winter dress—7. Rifleman with snow mask and clothing—8. Winter dress for sentries—9. Airman—10. Sergeant (air force)

11. German steel helmet, 1916 pattern—12. German steel helmet, 1935 pattern—13. Finnish steel helmet, introduced during the war—14. German steel helmet, 1935 pattern, decorated with the insignia of the 4th Kevyt Osasto (light detachment) in 1939–40. Steel helmets captured from the Russians were also worn. All these various types were in service at the same time, sometimes even within the same single unit.

---

1 One must be careful not to confuse the two meanings of the word 'Finnish'. In one sense it means the inhabitants of Finland and anything that relates to that country; in the other sense, it means the Finnish language and those who speak it. In Finland, nine-tenths of the population speak Finnish and the rest Swedish. There are even two names for the country: Suomi in Finnish and Finland in Swedish.

1   2   3   4   5

11   12   13   14

6   7   8   9   10

THE FIRST RUSSO-FINNISH WAR

It was on 1 December that the Soviet armed forces crossed stubborn little Finland's frontier in six places simultaneously, spread out over a distance of 1,000 miles. Around half a million men, among whom the Mongolian troops were the best trained for winter warfare, struck out at the Finnish positions. The Finns had only one ally: the winter, which was particularly cold at the end of 1939.

The 300,000 soldiers of Marshal Mannerheim had to cover every front. Seven Finnish divisions faced eight Russian divisions in the Karelian Isthmus, Finland's 'shield', with its famous Mannerheim line.[1] On the immense front, which ran from Lake Ladoga to the Arctic Ocean, three Finnish divisions opposed seven Soviet divisions.

In the south the system of fortifications successfully withstood formidable attacks on 10 and 19 December; in the east and north the Soviets had no more success and tramped around in this region of lakes and forests, harassed by an elusive enemy who continually launched the redoubtable skiers of the 'death patrols' against the Russian rear areas.

With bated breath the whole world followed the unfolding of this David and Goliath struggle. People were overjoyed when the emboldened Finns went over to the counter-attack in January 1940, in temperatures that sometimes dropped to 50°C below zero. The Soviets suffered extremely heavy losses, and the region of Suomussalmi alone was so strewn with corpses that it became known as the 'land of the dead man'. The booty was huge: in the village of Raate alone, the Finns captured 42 tanks, 10 armoured cars, 278 lorries, 102 guns and more than 1,000 prisoners.

This paradoxical turn of events was prematurely interpreted as an illustration of the prodigious strength of fortified lines and as obvious proof of the poor quality of the Soviet troops and leadership. Hitler was the first to make such an error, but he was not alone in being deceived. It is generally forgotten that the great Winston Churchill himself declared on the radio:[2] 'Finland had exposed, for the world to see, the military incapacity of the Red Army'.

There was to be a rude awakening, although these initial ideas were not immediately dispelled. By this time exhausted, the Finnish Army could not withstand a new offensive, which had been prepared more carefully, and was forced to capitulate on 12 February after a struggle lasting 104 days.

THE SECOND RUSSO-FINNISH WAR

With the launching of 'Operation Barbarossa' by the Germans, Finland firmly declared her intention to remain neutral. However, Soviet artillery bombardments of positions in the south of the country led eventually to a Finnish counter-stroke, which was put into operation under the command of Marshal Mannerheim from 25 June 1941 onwards. The latter nevertheless managed to preserve his independence *vis-à-vis* the German High Command. Great Britain was the only Allied country to declare war on Finland but this remained little more than a symbolic gesture. Having recovered the territories lost in 1940, Finland tried without success to open peace negotiations with the Soviet Union. In 1944 the victorious Russian offensive led President Ryti to call for German help on his own initiative; then, once the front had been re-established, to renounce his title which was subsequently bestowed on Marshal Mannerheim.

The peace agreement was signed on 19 September 1944. Once more, Finland lost the territories exacted by the Soviet Union in 1940, as well as the town of Petsamo. In addition, she had to pay a war indemnity of three hundred million dollars.

[1] Constructed with the help of Belgian engineer officers.

[2] Speech broadcast on the BBC on 20 January 1940.

UNIFORMS AND EQUIPMENT

In 1939 two types of uniforms were in use. These were the 1927 pattern uniform of chocolate-brown colour and the blue-grey 1936 pattern uniform. The helmets, which were mostly of German origin and of two types – the 1916 and 1935 patterns – were partly replaced by the purely Finnish helmet towards the end of the war. The same was true of equipment.[1]

The Finnish ski deserves a special mention here. Used in a masterly fashion, following a method which closely resembled Norwegian *orientiring*, this sturdy, cross-country ski was particularly adaptable for rapid journeys across snow-covered plains. Thinner and narrower than the Norwegian ski, the Finnish ski, called a *lapika*, was fastened by means of a simple strap which, although held in position by the curious turned-up toes of the special boots, also facilitated speedy removal when the occasion demanded.[2]

Weapons were of the most oddly assorted types and, to a large extent, were captured from the enemy as this summary shows:

	WAR OF 1939–40	WAR OF 1941–44
Tanks	Vickers-Armstrong 6 and 8 ton Mk E, Types A and B	Vickers-Armstrong 6 and 8 ton; Soviet BT 5 and 7, KV I and II
Aircraft	Bristol Bulldog Mk IV, Fokker D XXI, Gloster Gamecock II, Gloster Gladiator	Brewster 239, Curtiss Hawk 75A, Fiat 650, Hawker Hurricane I, Messerschmitt Me. 109 G2 and 6, Fokker D XXI, Fokker C V and C X, Gloster Gladiator, Westland Lysander, Bristol Blenheim, Junkers Ju. 88 A4, Dornier Do. 172
Artillery	75mm: Norwegian, Swedish, American, German and Russian (both Czarist and Soviet) 105mm: French 4.5in (114mm): British 120mm: Belgian and Russian (both Czarist and Soviet) 122mm: Russian (both Czarist and Soviet) 150mm: German 155mm: French 203mm: American, etc.	

---

[1] The Finnish Navy is dealt with in the general chapter on the navies of various fighting powers.

[2] From the sixth century onwards at least, the ski became an essential part of the life of the Finns. The Byzantine historian Procope gave them the name of 'Skidfinns'.

PART THREE

ITALY AND THE AXIS SATELLITES

The Italian Army

'*Le stellette sono disciplina di noi solda*' ('The little stars are the symbols of our soldiers' discipline') says a popular song. In spite of their modest size, the tiny stars which adorned the collar patches of the entire army represented one of the most typical elements of the Italian uniform. Their precise origin is uncertain. It would seem that the five-pointed star had appeared on the epaulettes of the Kingdom of Italy at the time of the Napoleonic conquest. Missing from uniforms for more than half a century, it re-appeared in 1871 by decree of the *Giornale militare*. At that period, the star was in white fabric for other ranks and embroidered for officers. Later on it was to assume its final form in embossed or stamped metal.

The uniform of the land army was of the same pattern for all and comprised: a grey-green tunic and trousers; puttees of the same colour which were bound round the trousers; and a very distinctive field cap (or side cap) which was in general use, but which officers could replace with an elegant flat peaked cap.

Certain formations, such as the Alpini (mountain troops) and Bersaglieri (special light infantry), wore special headgear to single them out from this uniformity. The Alpine troops instead wore the soft felt mountain hat with a straight feather stuck in it, while the Bersaglieri, on the eve of the war itself, still wore the broad-brimmed felt hat embellished with its splendid plume of cock feathers, a symbol which had made them famous since the Crimean War through a long history that included the taking of Rome in 1870, the First World War and the campaign in Ethiopia from 1935 to 1936.

The twelve Bersaglieri regiments had only been incorporated into the Italian infantry in 1940; they subsequently enjoyed the particular attention of the *Duce* himself, for Mussolini had served in their ranks during the First World War.

As a special privilege the two corps mentioned above wore the feather or the plume of which they were so proud on the steel helmet which, in 1935, had replaced the old model previously in service.

THE HELMET

The modern helmet bore a spherical bomb (or grenade) and did not have a prominent rim; painted grey-green, it also carried the insignia of the appropriate arm of service outlined in black stencil.

As an economy measure the French Adrian-type helmet was still largely used by second-line units, including:

Gunners of the anti-aircraft defence units
Fascist Militia of the anti-aircraft defence
Gunners and sailors of the anti-aircraft and coast defence artillery
Territorial troops
Air-Raid Wardens (U.N.P.A.), etc.

THE 'MOSTRINE'

The *mostrina*, the collar patch peculiar to Italian troops, varied according to the regiment and arm of service in question.

The infantry wore a divisional patch which served for two regiments. In certain cases, such as that of the motorised infantry divisions, the *mostrina* was supplemented by another *mostrina* of smaller dimensions so that its individual identity could be clearly defined. A few examples of this method will be seen in the illustrations.

TROPICAL DRESS

As a rule the troops fighting in Africa wore a uniform of an olive-khaki shade and of which the Saharan or desert tunic was adorned with the traditional *mostrine*, or collar patches. It seems likely, however, that the infantry, particularly the other ranks, did not wear these collar patches and that in the last stages of the campaign this lack of distinctive emblems spread throughout the army, since no more could be obtained in Italy because of the growing difficulties of the supply services.

It was not unusual to see soldiers clad in hybrid uniforms which combined olive-khaki and grey-green garments through sheer necessity.

The very fine tropical or colonial helmet, decorated with the regimental badge in metal and with the national cockade, was only issued to a few élite units. In the case of the Bersaglieri it was also adorned with the famous bronze colour plume.

THE CAVALRY

The fourteen cavalry regiments could be differentiated by their particular collar patches and by the emblems painted on their helmets: a black cross for the first four regiments; two crossed lances surmounted by the royal crown for the lancers; and a horn surmounted by a crown for the light horse.

The leather-trimmed riding-breeches were worn instead of trousers, with leggings for other ranks and with high boots for the officers.

The shabraque or saddle-cloth for officers was of short black fur and was provided with two saddlebags. The other ranks had a long-haired shabraque without saddlebags.

The regulation cavalry sabre was the 1871 model. However, some officers, having broken their own, replaced them with weapons captured from the enemy. Thus in Russia superb Cossack shashkas appeared, looking strangely anachronistic in the hands of their new owners.

This curious custom, one might almost say privilege, did not originate during the campaign in Russia; indeed, it had already been adopted during the operations in East Africa, when the present curator of the Cavalry Museum at Pinerolo rode about at the head of his troops armed with an impressive Abyssinian scimitar!

The horse furniture presented two quite extraordinary features. The first consisted of a leather collar worn around the horse's neck. When riding three abreast, the riders in the outer files could quickly hitch their mounts to those in the central file by means of this curious collar. They could therefore dismount to fight on foot, while their horses were literally held on a leash by their comrades in the central file who remained in the saddle. It goes without saying that this procedure was reserved for other ranks, as was the second peculiarity: a special extendible stirrup which unfolded to form another lower stirrup, thus making it easier for a heavily laden rider to climb into the saddle.

The officer's horse alone had a forelock and mane. Both were completely shaved on the horses ridden by other ranks.

We should not leave the subject of Italian cavalry without mentioning the unexpected honour which the fortunes of war granted this arm: that of making the last cavalry charge in history!

It was at Ischbuchensky, in Russia, on 24 August 1942, that the *Raggruppamento a cavallo* (Special Cavalry Group) of the *Armata Italiana (in) Russia* (AMIR, or Italian Army in Russia), which comprised the Novara and Savoia regiments, was able to take part in this final demonstration in the classic style determined by centuries of tradition. In fact, although the lancers of the Novara regiment managed to make a breach in the lines of Soviet infantry, the honours of the day belonged, above all, to the Savoia dragoons, following their action around this little village on the right bank of the Don.

While the Russian infantrymen opened up a merciless fire from their automatic weapons, the squadrons of the *Savoia Cavalleria*, led by their white-gloved officers, attacked them with their sabres in traditional fashion. The victory seriously damaged the ranks of the Savoia regiment and several of its best officers were mortally wounded; however, this memorable day had, for a while, relieved an extremely critical situation.

In his highly detailed account of the charge,[1] Lieutenant-Colonel V. Gibellini, the historian and outstanding military artist relates the touching story of a horse which had survived the slaughter. Relegated to the sad role of a cart-horse, the animal was recognised by a veteran of the Savoia regiment and responded when his name Albino, was called. The poor beast was soon given a home by the regiment, with whom it peacefully lived out its days, duly given a pension by the government.

For the operations in Russia the Italian Army had to equip itself with clothing capable of withstanding the terrible severity of the Russian winter. Somehow or other they succeeded and often rigged themselves out in non-regulation equipment, such as the cap shown in the illustrations.[2]

SMALL ARMS

In 1938 work had begun on the conversion of the old 6.5mm model 1891 rifle and 1891 carbine, or *moschetto*, into 7.35mm weapons of the Spitz type. However, events made it impossible to see this work through, even as far as the establishment of stocks of the new cartridges.

The two types of arms were nevertheless used simultaneously, although the 6.5mm was the predominant calibre. This was only one aspect of the general lack of organisation that characterised the Italian army at a time when the *Duce* launched it into a war that he believed could only be of short duration.

THE INTER-WAR PERIOD

In 1923 short-term military service of eight months was replaced by eighteen months' service.

The army could then count upon 400,000 recruits a year, at least in theory, but in fact the country's financial problems led the authorities to increase the number of exemptions. It can be estimated that at best the number of troops barely reached 300,000 men. Mussolini's accession to power gave him the opportunity to rectify this situation to some extent.

In 1930 Italy could deploy an army of 462,000 men, although one must include in this number the battalions of Blackshirts, a pair of which were introduced into each infantry division that same year. Counting the permanent Fascist formations, the Royal Carabinieri (select corps of military police) and the troops stationed in Libya, the available manpower reached 600,000 combatants. However, it would be wrong to assume that such diverse elements always got on well with each other. Time only aggravated the inevitable disagreements between professional soldiers and the 'amateur' militiamen who had the temerity to become involved in such a highly specialised profession.

ITALIAN ARMY I

1–2. Types of field equipment—3. Standard field dress—4. Hybrid uniform as worn in Africa. The old pattern steel helmet was no longer worn by first-line troops—5. Bersagliere (sharpshooter). The breeches could be of the type worn by the Metropolitan Army, as shown here, or in cotton khaki for Africa—6. Member of the Alpini and variations in the collar between 1940 (left) and 1941–45 (right)—7. Non-regulation dress as worn in Russia—8. Trooper of the Savoia cavalry regiment. Note the folding stirrup which was typical of the Italian cavalry, officers apart.—9. Corporal of the Savoia regiment

10. 6.5mm Mannlicher-Carcano *moschetto* (carbine), 1891 model, and 7.35mm carbine, model 1891–1938—11. 6.5mm Mannlicher-Carcano or Carcano-Parravicino rifle, model 1891–1938—12. 6.5mm Breda light machine-gun, model 1930—13. Carbine used by the Balilla or Fascist Youth. It was never a weapon of war—14. 9mm Beretta sub-machine-gun or machine-carbine, model 38A—15. 9mm Beretta automatic pistol, model 1934—16. 8mm Beretta medium machine-gun, model 1937

---

1 'Tradition', the Journal of the International Society of Military Collectors, No. 46.
2 The uniforms of the Italian Army after 1943 will appear in vol. 4.

It was with these troops that the Italian dictator, to avenge the disaster of Aduwa (1886), embarked on the conquest of Ethiopia in 1936. The following year, he found a new field for experiment in Spain, where 40,000 volunteers fought alongside General Franco's forces.[1]

ITALIAN ARMY II

Rank Insignia: 1. Marshal—2. Cap badge (on a red background for general officers) and collar insignia for staff officers: (a) Characteristic collar insignia; (b) General staff corps; (c) Staff officer of the 48th infantry division; (d) Non-divisional staff (engineers)—3. General—4. Lieutenant-General—5. Major-General—6. Brigadier-General—7. Colonel—8. Lieutenant-Colonel—9. Major—10. First Captain (primo capitano)—11. Captain—12. First Lieutenant (primo tenente)—13. Lieutenant—14. Second Lieutenant—15. Officer Candidate. The shoulder straps shown in the right hand column were worn on tropical dress.

16. Each infantry division could be identified by its own particular collar patch (*mostrina*) as in (a) measuring 60 × 32mm. It was also worn in combination with the particular insignia of the arm of service (b, d), in this case that of the 34th artillery regiment (the yellow should be orange) on the *mostrina* of the 64th Division (see following page).—17 a. Engineers' insignia; b. The same on the *mostrina* of the 33rd infantry division; c. Insignia of a staff officer in the 64th division—18 a. Territorial formations; b. Alpine garrison troops; c. Mobile territorial troops—19 a. Divisional artillery; b. 33rd infantry division (standard); c. Armoured division (the yellow should be orange)—20 a. Medical service; b. Medical service of the 33rd infantry division; c. Headdress insignia worn by doctors (the wings should be replaced by a five-pointed star); d. Pharmacists—21. Commissariat service—22. Veterinary service—23. Supply service—24. Customs (or finance guards)—25. Administration—26. Infantry tanks—27. Cavalry tanks—28. Motor transport corps—29. Chemical warfare branch: a. Headdress badge; b. Collar patch

Headdress insignia: 30. Artillery—31. Army corps artillery—32. Army artillery. The regimental number was inscribed in the central circle—33. Cavalry division artillery—34. Anti-aircraft artillery—35. Fortress artillery—36. Coast artillery—37. Railway artillery

Cavalry headdress insignia: 38. Lancers—39. Dragoons—40. Light horse. The regimental number was inscribed in the central circle—*Collar insignia of cavalry regiments:* 41 a. 1st—Nizza; b. 2nd—Piemonte; c. 3rd—Savoia; d. 4th—Genova; e. 5th—Novara (lancers); f. 6th—Aosta (lancers); g. 7th—Milano (lancers); h. 9th—Firenze (lancers); i. 10th—Vittorio Emmanuele II (lancers); j. 12th—Saluzzo (light horse); k. 13th—Monferrato (light horse); l. 14th—Alessandria (light horse); m. 19th—Guide (light horse); n. Cavalry school and depots (the yellow should be orange)

Headdress insignia: 42. Sappers—43. Telegraphists—44. Miners—45. Radio Telegraphists—46. Bridging engineers—47. Railway engineers

---

1 See also the chapter on Italian armoured fighting vehicles.

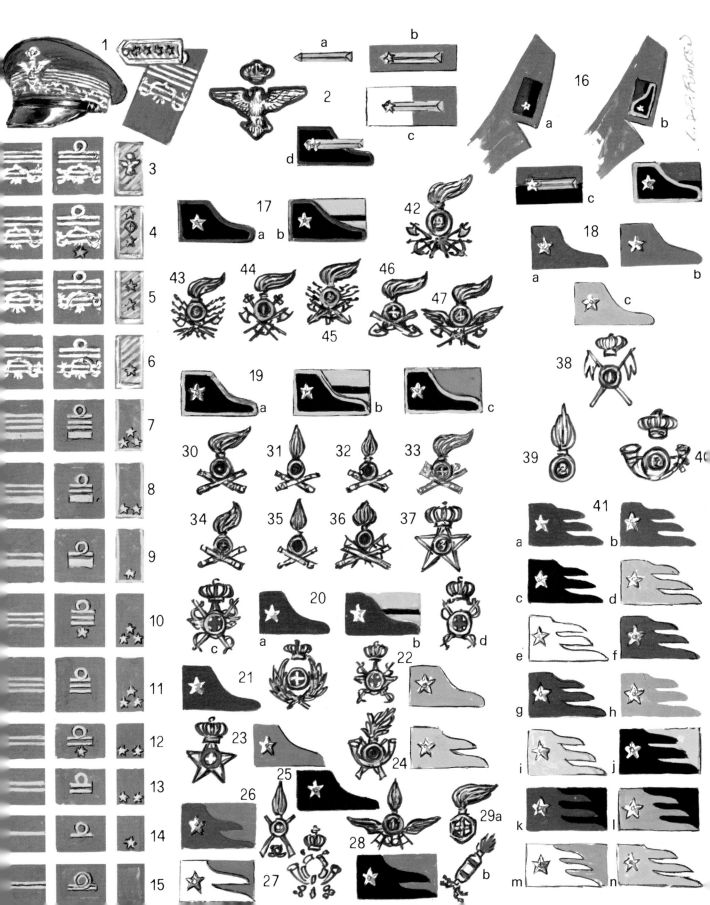

1. Private 1st Class (appuntato)—2. Lance-Corporal—
3. Corporal—4. Sergeant—5. Sergeant-Major—6. Company
Sergeant-Major (maresciallo ordinario)—7. Regimental
Sergeant-Major (maresciallo capo)—8. Warrant Officer (or
Adjutant)—9. Field cap worn by senior NCOs and Warrant
Officers. The twists in the yellow wool stripe become less
and less compact as the rank becomes higher—10–11. The
tie, normally grey-green in colour, was blue for the 73rd and
74th infantry regiments and red for the 1st, 2nd, 157th and
158th infantry regiments and the Savoia cavalry regiment—
12. Infantry headdress insignia—13. *Mostrina* (collar patch)
of a standard infantry division, in this case the 13th infantry
division—14. Motorised infantry division—15. Non-divisional infantry—16. Frontier guard infantry—17. Grenadiers
—18. Carabinieri. The special stripes are also worn length-
wise on the collar—19. Bersaglieri—20. Alpini (Alpine
infantry)—21. Alpine engineers—22. Alpine artillery—
23. Machine-gunners—24. Marine infantry (San Marco
marine regiment)

25. Collar patches or *mostrine* of infantry divisions and
regiments: 1st row, left to right: 13th div. (1st and 2nd inf.
regts) 29th div. (3rd and 4th inf. regts) 28th div. (5th and
6th inf. regts) 6th div. (7th and 8th inf. regts); 2nd row: 50th
div. (9th and 10th inf. regts) 56th div. (11th and 12th inf.
regts) 24th div. (13th and 14th inf. regts) 55th div. (15th and
16th inf. regts); 3rd row: 33rd div. (17th and 18th inf.
regts) 27th div. (19th and 20th inf. regts) 44th div. (21st and
22nd inf. regts) 14th div. (23rd and 24th inf. regts); 4th row:
15th div. (25th and 26th inf. regts) 17th div. (27th and 28th
inf. regts) 26th div. (29th and 30th inf. regts) 51st div. (31st
and 32nd inf. regts); 5th row: 4th div. (33rd and 34th inf.
regts) 16th div. (35th and 36th inf. regts) 3rd div. (37th and
38th inf. regts) 25th div. (39th and 40th inf. regts); 6th row:
37th div. (41st and 42nd inf. regts) 36th div. (43rd and 44th
inf. regts) 50th div. (45th and 46th inf. regts) 23rd div.
(47th and 48th inf. regts); 7th row: 49th div. (49th and 50th
inf. regts) 22nd div. (51st and 52nd inf. regts) 2nd div.
(53rd and 54th inf. regts) 32nd div. (55th and 56th inf. regts);
8th row: 10th div. (57th and 58th inf. regts) 31st div. (59th
and 60th inf. regts) 102nd div. (61st and 62nd inf. regts)
59th div. (63rd and 64th inf. regts); 9th row: 101st div.
(65th and 66th inf. regts) 58th div. (67th and 68th inf. regts)
61st div. (69th and 70th inf. regts) 38th div. (71st and 72nd
inf. regts); 10th row: 57th div. (73rd and 74th inf. regts)
54th div. (75th and 76th inf. regts) 7th div. (77th and 78th
inf. regts) 9th div. (79th and 80th inf. regts); 11th row:
52nd div. (81st and 82nd inf. regts) 19th div. (83rd and 84th
inf. regts) 60th div. (85th and 86th inf. regts) 20th div. (87th
and 88th inf. regts); 12th row: 5th div. (89th and 90th inf.
regts) 1st div. (91st and 92nd inf. regts) 18th div. (93rd and
94th inf. regts) 46th div. (95th and 96th inf. regts); 13th row:
97th and 98th infantry regts, 103rd div. (111th and 112th
inf. regts) 62nd div. (115th and 116th inf. regts) 45th div.
(125th and 126th inf. regts); 14th row: 41st div. (127th and
128th inf. regts) 47th div. 139th and 140th inf. regts) 64th
div. (141st and 142nd inf. regts) 12th div. (151st and 152nd
inf. regts); 15th row: 63rd div. (157th and 158th inf. regts)
48th div. (207th and 208th inf. regts) 53rd div. (225th and
226th inf. regts) 11th div. (231st and 232nd inf. regts)

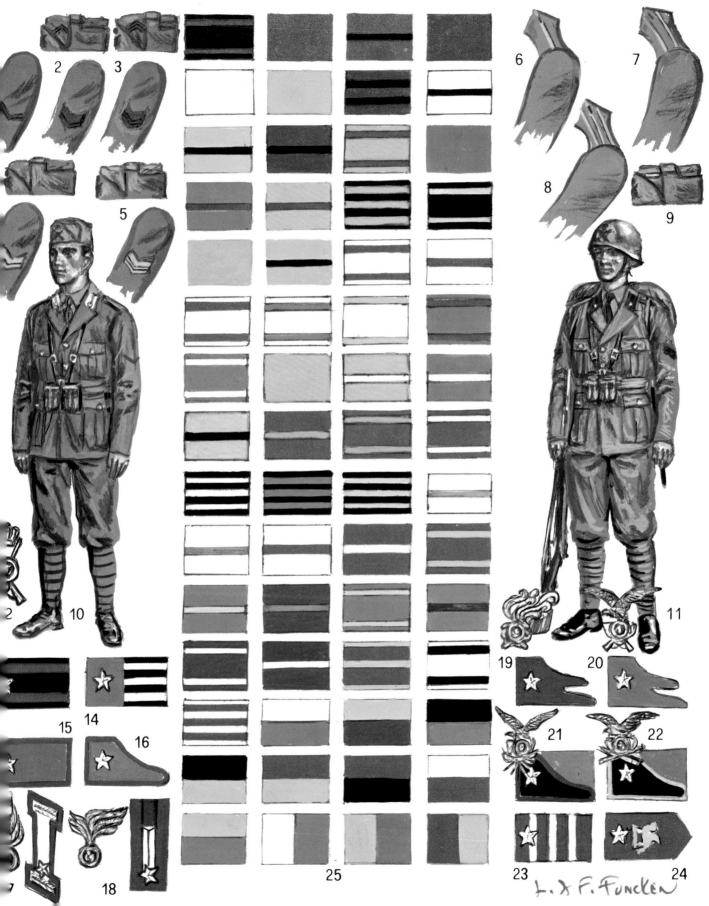

2　3　5　6　7　8　9

2　10　11

14　15　16

18

19　20　21　22　23　24

25

L. & F. Funcken

The Blackshirts

It was in Milan, on 23 March 1919, that Benito Mussolini, created the *Fasci di combattimento*. These combat groups, whose name calls to mind the *fasces* which were borne in front of the magistrates of ancient Rome to symbolise their authority, served as the foundation for a political movement, Fascism.

From 108 in 1920, the number of *Fasci* had climbed to 1,600 in 1921. By the end of the same year the militarisation of the Fascist party was complete and the *squadre*, or combat groups, became a real army: the Militia.

The first uniform to appear was comprised of a black shirt, grey-green breeches with a double black stripe down each side, and leggings. Every means possible of recalling the glories of ancient Rome was employed. Thus the Militia was divided into legions and not into regiments; the traditional battalions became cohorts, themselves sub-divided into centuries; while the front-line units of the Militia were called *principi* and those of the reserve were known as *triari*. It should also be remembered that the parade step of the Fascist troops, although inspired by the German 'goose-step', was christened the 'Roman step'.

Even the system of ranks did not escape this 'Romanisation'. Below is a list of these ranks, together with their equivalents in the Royal Army and the British Army.

FASCIST MILITIA	ROYAL ARMY	BRITISH ARMY
————	Generale di divisione	Major-General
Console generale	Generale di brigata	Brigadier-General
Console	Colonnello	Colonel
Primo seniore	Tenente colonnello	Lieutenant-Colonel
Seniore	Maggiore	Major
	Primo capitano	
Centurione	Capitano	Captain
	Primo tenente	
Capo manipolo	Tenente	Lieutenant
Sottocapo manipolo	Sottotenente	Second-Lieutenant
Aspirante sottocapo manipolo	Aspirante	Officer Candidate (no exact equivalent)
Primo aiutante	Maresciallo maggiore	Staff Sergeant-Major or Senior Warrant Officer
Aiutante capo	Maresciallo capo	Regimental Sergeant-Major
Aiutante	Maresciallo ordinario	Company Sergeant-Major
Primo capo squadra	Sergente maggiore	Sergeant-Major
Capo squadra	Sergente	Sergeant
Vicecapo squadra	Caporale maggiore	Corporal
Camicia nera scelta	Caporale	Lance-Corporal
Camicia nera	Appuntato	Private 1st Class (no exact equivalent)
	Soldato	Private 2nd Class (no exact equivalent)

ITALIAN ARMY, FASCIST FORMATIONS

1. Second-Lieutenant in field service dress with the Saharan tunic—2. Summer working dress—3. Capo manipolo (Lieutenant) in field dress—4. Centurione (Captain) of the forest Militia—5. Console Generale (Brigadier-General)—6. Primo capo squadra (Sergeant-Major)—7. Milite scelto (Corporal) of the forest Militia—8. Sottocapo manipolo (Second Lieutenant) of the M (Mussolini) battalion—9. Member of the *Moschettieri del Duce* (literally, The Duce's Musketeers)—10. Collar insignia (the *fasces*) which, in the case of the Fascist Militia, replaced the five-pointed star of the Royal Army

Collar insignia: 11. General (or combatant) Militia—12. Anti-aircraft and coast defence Militia—13. Frontier and forest Militia—14. Highway Militia

Rank insignia (worn on the cuff): 15. Gold braid on the grey-green uniform—On the black uniform: 16. Primo capo squadra (Sergeant-Major)—17. Capo squadra (Sergeant)—18. Vice-capo squadra (Corporal)—19. Camicia nera scelta (Lance-Corporal)—20. Capo squadra (Sergeant) in field dress

CREDERE OBBEDIRE COMBATTERE

1
2
3
4
5
6
7
8
9
10
11
12
13
14
15
16
17
18
19
20

On 15 December 1922, a few months after Mussolini had come to power, the Militia assumed its final form under the name of *Milizia Volontaria per la Sicurezza Nazionale* (Voluntary Militia for National Security) – or MVSN for short.[1]

Mussolini henceforth had his own Praetorian Guards, who were even exempt from taking the oath of loyalty to the King!

By 1933 there were nearly four million Fascists. The young were brigaded, whatever their age, into para-military organisations: at six a boy would join the *Balilla*;[2] from eight to twelve he would become a member of the *Balilla escursionisti* (raiders); from twelve to fourteen he would be in the *Balilla moschettieri* (musketeers), then the *avanguardisti* (vanguard) *moschettieri* from fourteen to sixteen, and the *mitraglieri* (machine-gunners) from sixteen to eighteen. The latter were tragically to follow, at Bir el Gobi, the second Commandment of the Fascist Decalogue: 'He who is not ready to give his body and soul to the Fatherland and to serve the *Duce* without question is not worthy of the Black Shirt'.

Italian Armoured Vehicles

The first Italian armoured forces appeared in 1918 under the name of *batteria autonoma carri d'assalto*. They included, in all, two 40-ton Fiat 2000s.[3] each armed with a 65mm gun and six machine-guns, and six small French Renault FT tanks. In 1921 the Fiat 3000, inspired by the Renault and designated the *carro armato modello* 1921, became the second type of Italian tank to take its place in the *batteria autonoma*.

An improved version, the Fiat 3000 B or *modello* 30, was built in 1930. However, the appearance in Britain of the new light tank developed by Carden-Loyd had the same effect in Italy as in many other countries, and the engineers immediately turned their attention to the problems of producing a

light tank. Entrusted to the firm of Ansaldo, this project gave birth, three years later, to the *carro veloce 33*. A better-armed model saw the light of day in 1935, and before long, a thousand examples of the first and second models, re-designated as the L3/33 and the L3/35, had been produced. The excellent performance of the *carro veloce* in Ethiopia encouraged Mussolini to employ them in Spain, where they were shared out in groups of fifty between the divisions of the Italian Legion.

After some initial successes with the Littorio division, disillusion with these armoured vehicles quickly set in. The *carro veloce* became bogged down in muddy ground because of the narrowness of its tracks and, even more serious, its armour could not withstand anti-tank shells, still less the fire of the Soviet T26 tanks used by the Republican forces.

On a tactical level, a new factor emerged: it was realised that it was impossible for a tank to occupy ground by itself. Without infantry support it became easy prey for men who were sufficiently

---

1 The uniforms of the Militia after 1943 will be shown in vol. 4.
2 Named after a young native of Genoa who gave the signal for the revolt against the Austrians in the eighteenth century.
3 The only two examples built.

ITALIAN ARMOURED FIGHTING VEHICLES I

1. L3/33 (1933)—2. L3/35 (1935) Both the armoured fighting vehicles shown in figs 1 and 2 are of the type *carro veloce leggero d'assalto* (fast light attack or assault tank)— 3. Fiat 3000/Model 1930 (or Fiat 3000B) of the type *carro di rottura* (breakthrough tank)—4. L6/40—5. M11/39— 6. M13/40—7. M14/41

8. Distinguishing symbols: Top left: tank of the commander of the 3rd battalion (3 companies). Top right: tank of the commander of the 1st battalion (2 companies). Command tanks bore the number of the battalion in Roman numerals. Below, first column: Command tank of the 1st company. Fourth tank of the 1st platoon of the 1st company. Third tank of the 2nd platoon of the 1st company. Second tank of the 3rd platoon of the 1st company. The distinguishing colour of the 1st company is red; the individual number of the platoon is indicated by one to three white stripes, with the tanks being numbered from 1 to 4 by platoon. The same system of identification applies to the 2nd company (blue), the 3rd (yellow) and the 4th (green). The command company of the battalion had black as its distinguishing colour, while white identified the command company of the regiment. In the latter case, the stripes identifying the platoons were in black.

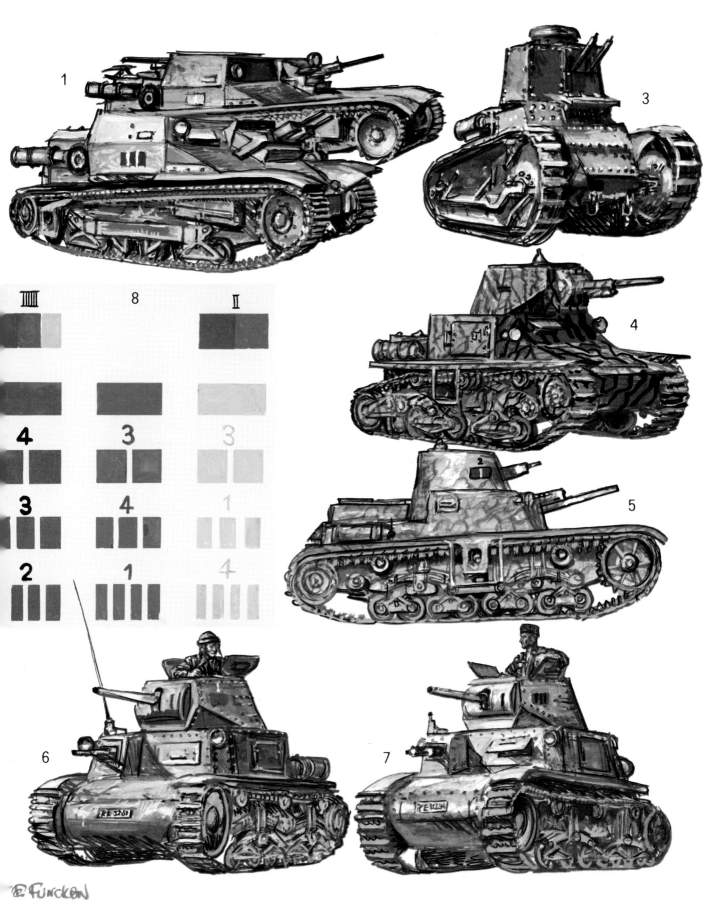

E. FUNCKEN

determined to attack it with incendiary projectiles, even comparatively primitive ones.

Re-organised into four *reggimenti fanteria carrista* (armoured infantry regiments), the Italian armoured forces did not suffer from the same mistakes in the invasion of Albania. This time, they were to benefit from the support of airborne troops.

In 1939 another type of tank, the *carro armato* M11/39, showed that it could stand comparison with foreign tanks of the same kind. An improved version of the L3, designated the L6/40, appeared at almost the same time.

Meanwhile, Italy had established her first *brigata corazzata* (armoured brigade), which comprised:

    1 tank regiment
    1 motorised Carabinieri regiment
    2 companies of 47mm anti-tank guns
    1 20mm anti-aircraft battery
    1 engineer company

In 1939 the existing armoured division made way for new formations, namely the Ariete, Centauro and Littorio armoured divisions.

Each of these three divisions contained:

    1 tank regiment with 4 battalions of 2 companies each
    1 Bersaglieri regiment
    1 motor-cycle battalion
    1 motorised battalion
    1 75mm motorised artillery regiment
    1 20mm anti-aircraft group
    1 engineer company

A fourth division, christened Celere, contained only one group of light tanks, two cavalry regiments, a regiment of Bersaglieri cyclists, a few motorised artillery pieces and a handful of auxiliaries. Obviously it was infinitely less formidable than the three preceding formations. However, even these units, in spite of all appearances, were to experience setbacks, as much from their weakness in tank strength, which was often reduced to two feeble battalions, as from the disastrous tactical use which was made of them in France as well as in Libya. In France, or rather at the French frontier, 550,000 Italians marked time while the tanks became entangled amongst the convoys, which were themselves trapped in the too-narrow valleys.

This was a far cry from the lightning war envisaged by the Italian dictator. To Marshal Badoglio, who had tried to dissuade him from attacking France, Mussolini had cynically replied: 'I need only a few thousand dead to enable me to sit as a belligerent at the peace conference table'.

He got his dead: 7,000 were killed, wounded or frozen for insignificant territorial gains. Of his troops, who had been pushed into this futile slaughter, Mussolini said: 'A people enslaved for sixteen centuries cannot become a conquering people in a few years'. In reality the dictator knew only too well that the vast majority of the Italian people did not want a war against France, and that for their part his troops were not inclined to sacrifice themselves needlessly when France was on the point of succumbing to the blows inflicted by the Wehrmacht. Besides, it has since been acknowledged that the French Chasseurs Alpins and the Italian Alpini were on the best of terms until 10 June 1940!

In Libya the Italian offensive had led to the capture of Sidi Barrani on 16 September. On 9 December a new tank, the M13, entered the lists. Then the blow fell: the British counter-attacked with such dash that on 10 December, at a cost of 476 dead, they took 130,000 prisoners, seized 237 guns and 200 lorries, and destroyed or captured nearly 500 tanks.

In spite of its marked superiority over previous models, the M13 could do nothing to avert this disaster, which could be attributed to lack of vigilance on the part of the Italian commanders and their failure to carry out adequate aerial reconnaissance. The technical inferiority and the lack of preparation of the armoured units had done the rest. After the German troops of the Afrika

ITALIAN ARMOURED FIGHTING VEHICLES II

1. M15/42—2. Semovente (self-propelled) Ansaldo-Fiat M13/40/41/42—3. P40—4. Autoblinda 40 (armoured car). Here the turret is shown turned to the rear—5. Autoblinda 41 (armoured car). The 'port-hole' type covers located on either side of the driver's position serve to protect the headlamps—6. Second-Lieutenant serving in infantry tanks

Korps had restored the situation, the first Italian tank to land in Africa was the M14/41, a variant of the M13/40 with a more powerful engine.

Another machine was to make a revolutionary appearance on the battlefield: this was the Semovente M13/40 armed with a 47mm anti-tank gun or a 75mm howitzer. This was undoubtedly the best of the Italian armoured fighting vehicles of the Second World War, even though it was used mainly as a self-propelled howitzer.

Finally, the last two tanks produced by Italy

SYNOPSIS OF ITALIAN ARMOURED FIGHTING VEHICLES FROM 1936 TO 1943

	TYPE	WEIGHT	ARMAMENT	CREW	SPEED	RANGE	SERVICE
Leggero d'assalto (light assault or attack tank)	L3/33	3.2 tons	1 8mm Breda 38 machine-gun	2	42 km/h	120 km	In Spain, Albania, Greece, Crete and in Russia with the Celere division
	L3/35	3.2 tons	2 8mm Fiat 35 machine-guns	2	42 km/h	120 km	Same use as the above; flamethrower and bridge-layer versions also existed
	L6/40	6.8 tons	1 20mm gun, 1 8mm machine-gun	2	42 km/h	200 km	Mainly used in North Africa, although some saw service in Russia
Medio di rottura (medium break-through tank)	M11/39	11 tons	1 37mm gun (model 37/40), 2 8mm Breda machine-guns	3	33 km/h	200 km	Africa: destroyed or captured; used by the 6th Australian cavalry regiment
Medio da combattimento (medium battle tank)	M13/40	14 tons	1 47mm gun (model 47/32), 3 8mm Breda 38 machine-guns	4	32 km/h	200 km	Africa, Balkans and Greece; destroyed at El Gazala after a desperate battle
	M14/41 (developed from the above)	14.5 tons	1 47mm gun (model 47/32), 3 8mm Breda 38 machine-guns	4	33 km/h	200 km	On the African front in 1942; El Alamein, then Tunisia in 1943; subsequently with the Fascist forces in Northern Italy
	M15/42 (developed from the above)	15.5 tons	1 47mm gun (model 47/40), 4 8mm Breda 38 machine-guns	4	40 km/h	220 km	Italy in 1943; then used by German parachute troops
Pesante da combattimento (heavy battle tank)	P40	26 tons	1 75mm gun (model 75/34), 1 8mm machine-gun	4	40 km/h	275 km	Seized by the Germans and used at Anzio
Semovente Ansaldo-Fiat (self-propelled gun: Ansaldo-Fiat)	M13/40 M14/41 M15/42	14.4 15 tons	1 75mm howitzer (or 1 75mm gun), 1 8mm machine-gun	3	35–40 km/h	200 km	Tripolitania and Tunisia in 1942, then Sicily, Sardinia and Italy; then used by the Germans

N.B. A certain number of French Somua and Renault 35 tanks, given up by France after the Armistice of 1940, were used in Sicily.

should also be mentioned: the M15/42, a more powerful version of the M14, and the P40, a *pesante da combattimento* (heavy battle tank), which was really a medium tank almost comparable in quality to the German Panzer IV. The P40s, which emerged from the factories in 1943, were only used in fact by the Germans, who seized them, along with all the other tanks in Italy, after their former ally had concluded an armistice on 8 September of that year.

Italy possessed three other types of armoured fighting vehicle, all based on the same initial model: the *auto-blindata* 40 of the armoured reconnaissance-vehicle type. The model AB40 had three 8mm machine-guns, the model AB41 a 20mm gun and an 8mm machine-gun, and the model AB43 a 47/40 gun and two 8mm machine-guns. All three carried a crew of four. The model AB40 weighed 6.48 tons, while the AB41 and AB43 each weighed 7.47 tons.

THE UNIFORM OF THE TANK CREWS

The uniform shown in the illustrations was that worn by officers from 1939 to 1943.

The black leather jacket was always worn, even in Africa, but in the latter case over linen garments, usually blue linen overalls such as those worn by mechanics. Rank badges were not supposed to appear on the leather jacket, but many officers wore them on the sleeves, such badges being made of thin plates or strips cut out of brass.

Only NCOs and men had the right to wear black leather leggings. Cavalry breeches were worn by everyone, but neither boots nor leggings were put on with overalls.

Contrary to popular belief, still current today, the Italian Army won the respect of its conquerors even when it suffered its heaviest defeats, as in Africa. The British paid tribute to the courage of the defeated Italians by granting them the honours of war after their surrender. The Italian soldier fought honourably, but without enthusiasm, in the *guerra dei poveri* (the poor people's war), into which he had been thrown by a dictator who was drunk with pride.

The Italian Air Force

After the First World War certain military thinkers had begun to develop new theories completely at odds with the official doctrines that regarded the teachings of 1914–1918 as definitive.

Major-General Giulio Douhet was one such thinker and, in 1921, he published his *Il Dominio dell' Aria* (The Command of the Air), which soon aroused impassioned reaction. A true prophet, this fifty-two year old Major-General foresaw not only the spectacular re-birth of militarism in Nazi Germany but also, most importantly, the decisive role of air power in the next 'total war', with its complete disregard of the safety of civilian populations. Douhet predicted the use of aircraft bristling with cannon and machine-guns, capable of carrying several tons of bombs and operating in perfect co-ordination with land and naval forces. In short, he foresaw *Blitzkrieg* warfare, in which tanks would play the minor, and aircraft the major and decisive part.

These predictions found little support however, and ten years later in spite of Mussolini's vigorous efforts, Italy herself could count on a *Regia Aeronautica* of only 1,200 aircraft, while France could line up some 1,650.

Admittedly Italy had made a special effort to equip herself with truly operational bombers, but only at the expense of her fighters, which to a large extent were still biplanes, or were not fitted with very powerful engines.

By the time she entered the war on 10 June 1940 Italy could pride herself on possessing, in numerical terms at least, one of the most impressive air forces in the world with its 5,000 aircraft, of which about 1,000 were bombers of a very high quality.

The fighters of this period showed the same

ITALIAN AIR FORCE II

1. Caproni Ca-135—2. Savoia-Marchetti SM 79-JR *Sparviere* (Hawk)—3. Savoia-Marchetti SM 79-JR—4. Fiat BR-20M *Cicogna* (Stork)—5. Piaggio P-108B—6. Wing insignia—7. Rudder insignia (the arms of the house of Savoy)—8. Fuselage insignia (*fasces*)—9. Air force officer—10–11. Parachutist and detail of collar patch

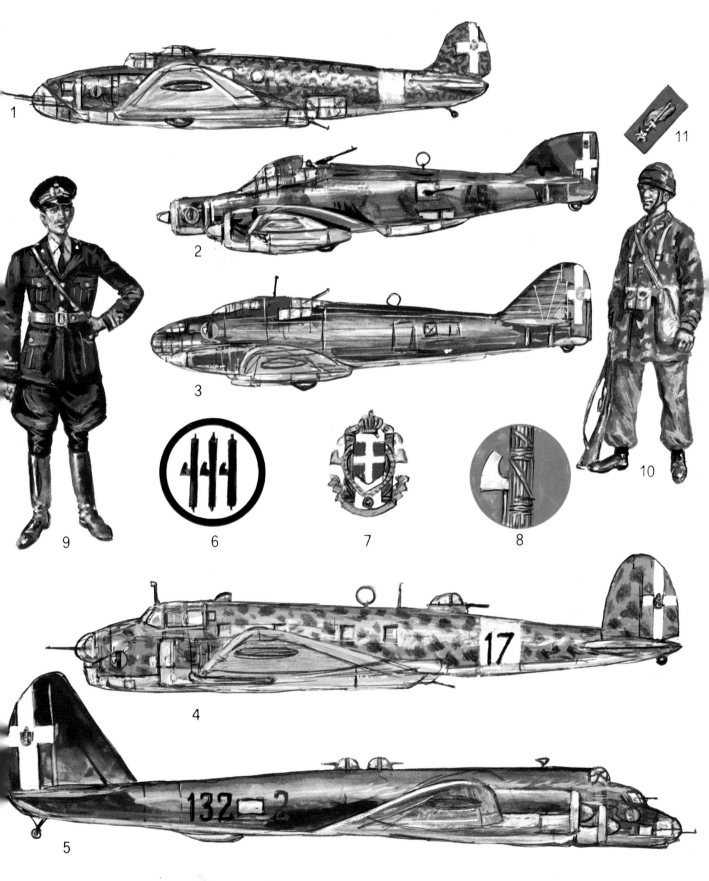

1

2

3

9

6

7

8

10

11

4

17

5

132 2

L. & F. Funcken

defects as those of ten years earlier. Typical was the Fiat CR32 biplane, of which nearly 800 examples were still in service, even though they had been relegated to second-line duties.

The CR42, younger brother of the CR32, was the world's last biplane fighter but, nevertheless, more than 1,700 were built from 1939 onwards. It had to be withdrawn from the Battle of Britain after two months of operations, which had proved extremely hazardous for such an obsolete biplane.

Among the more modern monoplane types, the Fiat G50 *Freccia* (Arrow) and its G50bis variant were widely used. However, because the G50 lacked adequate firepower, the Macchi C200 *Saetta* (Lightning), an exceptionally manoeuvrable monoplane, was generally preferred.

In 1942 and 1943, once the Italian fighters had been given more powerful engines, such as the German Daimler-Benz, some new and particularly successful types began to appear. The best was the powerful and streamlined Fiat G55 *Centauro* (Centaur), but the Italian surrender came just as its delivery to the squadrons was getting under way.

The Macchi C202 *Folgore* (Thunderbolt) was more fortunate. It began to roll off the production lines in 1941 and first saw combat in the skies of Libya, where it soon confirmed its clear superiority over the Hurricane and the Curtiss P40.

Also sent to Russia, the *Folgore* was to become the best of all the Italian fighters which were used on a large scale. Nearly 1,500 of them were built.

Another Macchi aircraft, the C205 V *Veltro* (Greyhound), a development of the *Folgore*, appeared in 1943. Only 70 were built, for the fateful date of 8 September cut short its production.

Similarly, other types which appeared belatedly suffered the same fate. These included the Reggiane Re2001 *Falco* II (Falcon II), Re2002 *Ariete* (Ram) and Re2005 *Sagittario* (Archer). Only some 250 of the first ever flew, while only 50 of the second and 48 of the last-named saw service.

After the surrender the pilots who were stationed in the area of Italy which had fallen into the hands of the Allies were allocated to Anglo-American squadrons. Their comrades in the north continued, whether they liked it or not, to fight for the ephemeral *Republica sociale italiana*, the last feudal stronghold of Fascism and a farcical and pathetic caricature of its former splendour.

Croatia

The Croats, although numbering 6,000,000, have always been a little-known people. This ignorance stems from the fact that for nearly a thousand years Croatia was always amalgamated with other more powerful states. After having been voluntary subjects of the sovereigns of the House of Hapsburg for five centuries they suffered the consequences of the Austro-Hungarian disaster of 1918 and became an integral part of Yugoslavia, then newly created by the Allies. Fierce defenders of their independence, the Croats tried to assert their claims but their parliament was dispersed and they were forced to submit whether they liked it or not.

The victory of the Axis forces in Yugoslavia

CROAT FORCES

1. Oustachi wearing the old Yugoslavian uniform but with the collar open in the German style—2. Bosnian—3-4. Officer and Private in German uniform—5. Airman wearing Luftwaffe uniform

Ranks: 6. General of infantry, cavalry and artillery (the third star is missing in this illustration)—7. Major-General—8. Brigadier-General—9. Colonel—10. Lieutenant-Colonel—11. Major—12. Captain (cavalry)—13. Lieutenant (supply)—14. Lieutenant (artillery)—15. Major (medical service)—16. Second Lieutenant (veterinary branch)—17. Second Lieutenant (military tribunal)—18. Officer Candidate (commissariat)—19. Sergeant (artillery)—20. Regimental Sergeant-Major (artillery)—21. Sergeant-Major (engineers: the three stars should be white)—22. Platoon leader—23. Corporal—24. Private 1st Class (artillery)—25. Private 2nd Class—26. Military Academy, Officer Cadet 1st Class—27. Military Academy, Officer Cadet 2nd Class—28. Pupil at NCOs' school

29. Arm badges—30. Detail of the star known as the *Dreiblat* (triple-leaf) which was in gold for staff officers or in plain white metal for NCOs.

7

8

9

10

12

13

14

15

17

18

19

20

30

1

2

3

4

5

.XFIGUNDEN

22

23

24

26

27

28

KROATIEN

HRVATSKA

29

provided the opportunity for the Oustachis,[1] a group of nationalist extremists, to restore the Croatian state in April 1941, with their chief, Ante Pavelic, at its head. Ten days after the Germans had launched their attack on the Soviet Union Pavelic called the Croatian volunteers to arms with the cry '*Za Dom*' (for the Homeland).

The first volunteers were assembled at Varasdin on the Drave and formed into two battalions. A third battalion, composed of Bosnians, gathered together at Sarajevo. The future Croatian air and naval forces assembled at Zagreb.

With drums beating, the organisation of this tiny army was soon proceeding at a brisk pace. The infantry, assembled in Austria, formed a reinforced regiment comprising three 3-company battalions, each equipped with 3 mortars and 12 machine-guns, a headquarters company with a signalling and liaison section, an engineer detachment, a few squadrons of cavalry, a company with 8 mortars and an anti-tank company. Next came the Bosnian battalion, the artillery detachment and the supply train. Music was not overlooked and the strains of the 'Varasdina' helped the volunteers along on their long march on foot towards the front, under the command of Colonel Markuij, on 22 August 1941. Having covered nearly 930 miles in a month, the Croatian regiment was then attached to the German 100th Light Division and was designated the 369th infantry regiment.

The Croats, like most of the other volunteer legions, were mainly employed in the war against partisans, a type of fighting in which their ancestors had already won fame in past centuries while serving under commanders such as Wallenstein, Prince Eugène, von Schlichting or Frederick the Great of Prussia.

Then came the classic engagements at Kharkov, Voronej, Kalatch and on the Don, followed by the bloody actions at Proletskultura and the hell of Stalingrad when the only remaining battalion fought in the Red October factory. Two more

---

1 Members of the Oustacha, a secret society which made itself known in the West by the assassination of King Alexander I of Yugoslavia at Marseilles on 9 October 1934.

legions appeared later in the Balkans: one finally joined Tito's ranks and the other surrendered to the Russians.

UNIFORMS

Wholly German apart from the collar patches, the uniforms also bore the national shield emblem.

The air force wore Luftwaffe uniforms with a small winged badge in the national colours which was fastened to the breast above the German eagle. The distinctive colours varied only for pilots (pale blue), auxiliaries (light grey) and the medical service (brown).

After having seen action in Russia, the Croatian airmen began to desert from 1943 onwards and ended up by fighting their former ally.

Bohemia-Moravia and Slovakia

After the final splitting up of Czechoslovakia on 14–15 March 1939,[2] what had hitherto re-

2 See 'Czechoslovakia' in vol. 1, page 92.

BOHEMIA–MORAVIA

Rank insignia (worn on collar patches): 1. General—2. Colonel—3. Lieutenant-Colonel—4. Major, 1st Class—5. Major—6. Captain—7. Lieutenant—8. Second-Lieutenant—9. Regimental Sergeant-Major—10. Company Sergeant-Major—11. Sergeant-Major—12. Sergeant. The collar patch of a Corporal bore two stars in white metal arranged in a fashion similar to the two silver stars worn by a Company Sergeant-Major (fig. 10).

Rank insignia (worn on the shoulder straps): 13. Junior Officer, with battalion number—14. Staff or Field Officer, with number of inspectorate board—15. Staff Officer, Inspectorate-General—16. General

Shoulder strap insignia for 1st Class Officers: 17. Officer—18. Senior Commissariat Officer—19. Military Auditor (paymaster's branch)—20. Doctor (medical branch)—21. Officers' cap badge

22. Private in marching order—23. Officer in marching order—24. Officer in field service cap—25. General in greatcoat (evening dress)—26. General in parade dress

mained of her territory was now split up into two distinct political entities: one was Slovakia, which became a German satellite state with Mgr Tiso at its head, and the other was the Protectorate of Bohemia–Moravia, in which President Hacha was directly subordinate to a *Reichsprotektor*. In this case, the role of 'Protector' was entrusted in 1941 to Reinhard Heydrich, who had had a brilliant career in the German police.

In his detailed account of the assassination attempt of the *Reichsprotektor* in Prague on 27 May 1942, Alan Burgess[1] emphasises the degree of influence achieved by the 'insistent, insidious and constant' Nazi propaganda on a population which had been forced to work entirely for the war effort of its new masters. Germany was filled with persistent but unverified reports about Czechoslovakia, which was described as a new 'land of plenty' where everybody had enough to eat. These stories contained some element of truth, for the shrewd Heydrich had conciliated the Czech workers by playing on their appetites when the normal ration was in fact far from being adequate. Those who worked overtime were paid with coupons for fats, meat and bread and the workers who showed themselves to be particularly keen were given paid holidays in the best hotels at health resorts. In a single month of this skilful blackmail, the production of the armaments factories had noticeably increased. It is necessary to bear in mind the terrible hardships suffered during that period to understand how the simple desire to eat can soon turn into an obsession.

In this way the *Reichsprotektor* was able to maintain his hold over the country. Each day more Czechs went over to the Nazis, a fact which did not escape the Czech Secret Service in London who decided to bring this disturbing situation to an abrupt and violent end.

The assassination of Heydrich by seven parachutists from different groups of saboteurs at large in Czechoslovakia resulted in terrible reprisals,[2] but it shook the edifice of the Nazi régime in that country and led not only to the Slovakian rising two years later, but also to the rising in Prague in 1945.

UNIFORMS

As early as 1939 forces were raised in the two states and were recruited mainly from the Czechs of German origin.

The uniforms issued were quite simply those of the old Czechoslovakian Army, to which new collar insignia or even a swastika armband was added. Sometimes the helmet also bore the Patriarchal cross, which was similar to the Cross of Lorraine. This emblem, however, only survived in the forces of the Slovak Legion, known also as the *Slowakien Schnelldivision*, which was raised in 1941 for the attack on Soviet Russia.

By that time the army of *Volkdeutsche* (ethnic Germans) of Bohemia–Moravia had been disbanded after its brief participation in the Polish campaign, and its members were then purely and simply absorbed into the Wehrmacht without keeping even the smallest item of insignia to recall their country of origin.

As for the uniforms of Czech origin which had been tolerated in the ranks of the Slovak Legion, these were soon replaced by the wholly German uniform, so that the only distinguishing feature was a sleeve badge in the national colours. It should be noted in passing that the same procedure was

1 *Seven Men at Daybreak.*
2 Hitler ordered that the village of Lidice should be razed to the ground, its men massacred and its women and children deported to concentration camps.

SLOVAKS

Rank insignia (worn on collar patches): 1. General, 1st Class—2. General, 2nd Class—3. Colonel (staff)—4. Lieutenant-Colonel (doctor)—5. Major (tanks or armoured forces)—6. Captain (legal or Judge-Advocate's branch)—7. Lieutenant (reconnaissance units)—8. Second-Lieutenant (quartermaster's or service branch)—9. Officer Candidate (cartographic or map-making branch)—10. Officer Cadet (secretariat)—11. Company Sergeant-Major (technical branch)—12. Sergeant-Major (medical branch)—13. Sergeant (air branch)—14. NCO Candidate, or Acting NCO (cavalry)—15. Reserve NCO candidate, or Acting reserve NCO (artillery)—16. Corporal (engineers)—17. Lance-Corporal (material or equipment branch)—18. Private, 1st Class (transport train)—19. Rifleman or Light Infantryman—20. Guard Infantry

21. Senior or Field Officer—22. Junior Cavalry Officer—23–24. Infantrymen—25. Private (engineers)—26–27. Headdress insignia

adopted for the French volunteers who, having left Versailles in civilian clothes, firmly believed that they would serve in French uniforms and became disenchanted when they realised too late that they were destined to wear the German field grey uniform.

The airmen were not exempt from this rule and wore the grey-blue uniform of the Luftwaffe.

THE SLOVAK AIR FORCE

The tiny Slovak air force took part in the attack on Poland. Organised under the benevolent patronage of the Luftwaffe and the energetic direction of the President-Prelate Tiso, the squadrons of the single Slovak air force regiment took off for the front. However, the two timid attacks delivered by unenthusiastic pilots, flying obsolete machines, did not contribute a great deal to the collapse of the Poles.

Somewhat under wraps in the year that followed, the Slovak air force was sent to Russia, but it had to be withdrawn in the winter of 1941 since its old aircraft proved unserviceable in the rigours of the Russian climate. The heat of combat did not lessen in any way and, in the Kiev sector, one fighter pilot even preferred to slip away towards the Russian lines.

Short of everything, even of training aircraft, the Slovak air force was obliged once more to make an appeal to the German Air Mission which had been established at Bratislava. Training machines were subsequently provided and the operational units strengthened with 12 modern bombers and 12 Me.109Es.

Formed in Germany from Slovak elements favourable to the 'New Order', No. 14 Group, equipped with Me.109Es, first saw action on the Eastern Front in 1942. Under the irresistible pressure of the Soviet forces, the fighter group was forced to abandon its base . . . and its aircraft were grounded for lack of fuel.

Re-equipped with the Me.109G, the unfortunate pilots were then attached to the Slovak Legion in the Crimean sector in 1943.

As the warning signs of the impending defeat of the Third Reich became increasingly clear the Slovaks began to desert on an ever-greater scale, either reaching the Russian lines or re-joining the Czech air force units fighting alongside the Anglo-Saxons. The national rising in Slovakia in August 1944 hastened the disintegration of all the squadrons, which took off to land on Soviet aerodromes or even turned round to fight against their former ally.

PART FOUR
THE NAVY AND NAVAL AIR ARMS

The War at Sea from 1939 to 1942

The very first naval battle of the Second World War was joined on 1 September 1939 by the tiny Polish fleet,[1] but it passed virtually unnoticed by the public at large whose attention was diverted by a much more spectacular event: the torpedoing of the British Liner *Athenia* on 3 September.

THE DRAMA OF THE ATHENIA

This torpedoing was the work of a German submarine and the feelings it aroused were similar to those stirred up by the sinking of the *Lusitania* during the First World War.

The first victim of the terrible Battle of the Atlantic, the *Athenia* was carrying 1,432 passengers; 112 of them perished of whom 28 were Canadians and Americans. A certain Jack Kennedy was to greet the survivors in Glasgow and conduct the investigation which his father, the United States Ambassador in Britain, had instructed him to carry out in order to establish the circumstances of the drama.

Energetically denying his country's involvement in such an unspeakable attack, Grand Admiral Raeder assured the Führer that no U-Boat had been less than 75 miles from the scene of the tragedy on that particular day. But when the submarine U-30 returned to Wilhelmshaven, her commander, Lieutenant Lemp, admitted to Admiral Dönitz that he had indeed sunk the *Athenia*; in the excitement of the first hours of the war he had mistaken her for an auxiliary cruiser. Subsequently assigned with his crew to the U-110,

Lieutenant Lemp disappeared in the Atlantic on 9 May 1941, taking with him the answer to the riddle on which the Nuremberg Tribunal was not able to shed any light.

This disastrous mistake was not to be the only one of its kind. On one occasion a U-Boat sank one of its own country's ships which was returning from Japan.[2]

THE ODYSSEY OF THE BREMEN

While the saga of the sinking of the *Athenia* was unfolding, another liner, the *Bremen*, the pride of the German merchant marine, had taken to the open sea. She had left New York after having been delayed for thirty-six hours by a painstaking search by American Customs officers. President Roosevelt maintained that this was in no sense a discriminatory measure, but the fact remains that her immobilisation had been turned to good account by a British cruiser, the *Berwick*, which had left the coast of Maine to intercept this magnificent transatlantic liner, a desirable prize for the Royal Navy.

The British Admiralty had deployed submarines and numerous other warships to lie in ambush.

1 See below: 'The Polish Navy'.
2 The submarines will be the subject of a special chapter in vol. 4.

THE FRENCH, BRITISH AND GERMAN NAVIES (pages 50–51)

1. The *Dunkerque* (France)—2. The *King George V* (Great Britain)—3. The *Leipzig* (Germany)—4. The *Dido* (Great Britain)—5. The *Repulse* (Great Britain)—6. The *Tirpitz* (Germany)—7. The *Scharnhorst* (Germany)—8. The *Nürnberg* (Germany)—9. The *Lorraine* (France)—10. The *Terrible* (France)—11. The *Lützow* (Germany)
Uniforms of the Royal Navy: 12. Commodore, 2nd Class—13. Commander in summer dress—14. Lieutenant-Commander in khaki service dress—15. Lieutenant in tropical dress—16. Junior Rating

6

7

8

14

9

6

10 12-

L.&F.FUNCKEN

11

16

However, Commodore Adolf Ahrens, the skipper of the *Bremen*, had decided to try everything to save his ship or to scuttle her without delay if he was checked.

Favoured by the bad weather, the *Bremen* made a dash to the north beyond the normal sea lanes, while the whole crew covered her with grey paint to make her less visible in the fog. Three days later the liner arrived without further trouble at Murmansk and from there reached Bremerhaven once again. She had won the game against the Royal Navy when few had doubted that her end was near. She was destroyed by fire in March 1941, almost certainly as a result of an act of sabotage.

THE TORPEDOING OF THE COURAGEOUS

On 18 September 1939 the Royal Navy's oldest aircraft carrier, which had been in reserve since 1917 and was now assigned to convoy protection duties, sank with a loss of 578 men. Her commanding officer, Captain W. T. Makeig-Jones, upheld the finest traditions of the Navy, as he calmly saluted the White Ensign until the waves engulfed him. The protection of convoys was to become a critical problem which the French and British Admiralties found increasingly difficult to solve.

THE BATTLE OF THE RIVER PLATE

The pocket battleship *Admiral Graf von Spee*, the last of a series of three 10,000-ton warships authorised by the Treaty of Versailles, was the principal actor in a new drama of the war at sea, which commenced on 17 December 1939.

Like her elder sister-ships, the *Deutschland* and the *Admiral Scheer*, the *Admiral Graf von Spee*, introduced into service in 1936, represented a real revolution in the art of of naval construction with her 11-inch guns mounted in two triple turrets, while no foreign cruiser of the same tonnage possessed guns bigger than 8-inch. Her welded hull relieved her of the weight of rivets and her radius of action was unparalleled.

The war began for the new *Panzerschiff* on 21 August 1939 when her captain, Hans Langsdorff, took her to sea for an 'unknown destination'. For a month the German raider was not mentioned. Admittedly Hitler hoped that his attack on Poland would not necessarily lead to a widening of the conflict – an opinion apparently confirmed by the hesitant attitude of the British and French in spite of their declaration of war on Germany.

It was only after his 'peace offensive' had failed that the Führer on 26 September 1939 ordered his surface raiders, the *Deutschland* and *Graf von Spee*, to emerge from their lairs.

The *Graf von Spee*'s first victim was an old British tramp steamer, the *Clement*, sunk by gunfire off Pernambuco on 30 September. Between that

GERMAN NAVY I

1. Captain's peaked cap—2. Cap worn by Lieutenants, Warrant Officers, Chief Petty Officers and Petty Officers, 1st Class—3. Cap of an Officer in the naval artillery—4–5. Junior Ratings' caps—6. Standard side (or overseas) cap, worn at sea (with gold piping for officers)—7–8. Steel helmets

Rank insignia (shoulder and sleeve): 9. Admiral—10. Vice-Admiral (medical)—11. Rear-Admiral (engineering)—12. Commodore (ordnance)—13. Captain (technical communications)—14. Commander (administration)—15. Lieutenant-Commander (defensive ordnance)—16. Lieutenant (naval coast artillery)—17. Sub-Lieutenant (communications reserve)—18. Ensign

Badges worn on the left sleeve of the white summer uniform (in yellow on the blue uniform): 19. Boatswain (seaman)—20. Signalman—21. Telegrapher—22. Carpenter—23. Ordnance Engineer—24. Torpedo Engineer—25. Mine Engineer—26. Yeoman (writer)—27. Pharmacist—28. Musician—29. Machinist—30. Radioman—31. Naval Artilleryman

Badges in red on blue background (in blue on the white uniform): 32. Anti-aircraft machine-gunner—33. Anti-aircraft machine-gun Crew Leader—34. Anti-aircraft Gunlayer (or Chief of anti-aircraft gun crew)—35. Gunlayer, Turret, with 3 years' service—36. Gunlayer, coast artillery—37. Gun Captain—38. Anti-aircraft gun Captain—39. Mechanical Engineering Instructor—40. Rangefinder Operator—41. Anti-aircraft Rangefinder Operator—42. Torpedo-tube Captain—43. Assistant Torpedo Instructor—44. Mine Captain—45. Bandsman (drummer)—46. Fire Controller—47. Diver—48. Deep-sea Diver—49. Hydrophone Operator—50. Anti-aircraft Sound Locator—51. Anti-aircraft Searchlight Operator—52. Electrical Motor Instructor—53. Athletics Instructor—54. Reserve Gunlayer—55. Reserve Minelayer

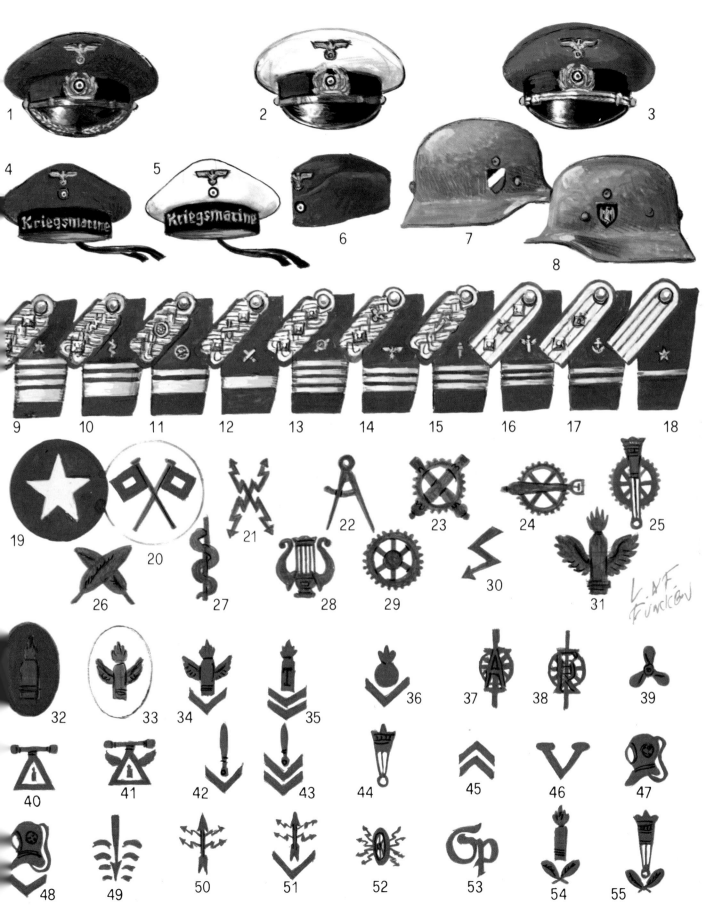

1

2

3

4

5

6

7

8

9 10 11 12 13 14 15 16 17 18

19

20

21

22

23

24

25

26

27

28

29

30

31

L.&F.
Funcken

32

33

34

35

36

37

38

39

40

41

42

43

44

45

46

47

48

49

50

51

52

53

54

55

date and 7 December the pocket battleship sank nine ships, but two of them had had time to send out distress calls giving their exact position. These signals were intercepted 3,000 miles away by the commander of the Royal Navy's South America Division, Commodore Harwood, who despatched three of his cruisers, *Exeter*, *Ajax* and *Achilles*, to intercept the raider *en route* for the estuary of the River Plate off the Uruguayan coast.

On 13 December the *Graf von Spee* fired the first rounds with her formidable 11-inch guns against the 8-inch guns of the *Exeter* and the relatively puny 6-inch guns of the smaller cruisers *Ajax* and *Achilles*. Happily for the British, the German battleship had to choose between three targets, while her assailants had only one target and a big one at that. Though the German gunners virtually silenced the turrets of the *Exeter* and *Ajax*, it is interesting to note that their 11-inch shells did not have the expected effect on the relatively light armour-plate of the British cruisers' hulls, which were considered barely capable of withstanding 8-inch shells. Finally, like a wild boar harried by hounds, the German raider sought refuge in the neutral waters of the Montevideo roads, while all available units of the Royal Navy hurried to the scene from all corners of the Atlantic.

The *Graf von Spee* was given a respite of seventy-two hours by the Uruguayan authorities to repair the damage caused by hits from twenty-seven British shells. The German losses had risen to thirty-six sailors, while four had been killed aboard the *Achilles*.

On 17 December the raider left her anchorage and stopped five miles out while boats were lowered. At 17.55 hours a series of explosions shook the ship, which sank slowly. She disappeared beneath the waves at 19.37.

Three days later Captain Langsdorff was found dead in an hotel room, stretched out on an old Imperial German Naval ensign bearing the Iron Cross motif. This gallant sailor had not wished to outlive the ship which he had scuttled on Hitler's orders. By a strange coincidence the newest of the Kriegsmarine's pocket battleships had ended her brief career not far from the spot where Count von Spee, the man to whom she owed her name, had lost his life twenty-five years earlier.

THE TRAGIC ADVENTURE OF THE BISMARCK

The drama of the River Plate action did not halt the *guerre de course* (raiding war) which the Germans had unleashed, particularly after their capture of Norwegian and French ports. On 23 October 1940 the pocket battleship *Admiral Scheer*, then, a month later, the heavy cruiser *Admiral Hipper* and finally in January 1941, the battleships *Scharnhorst* and *Gneisenau*, flung themselves into attacks on British convoys, sinking between them a total of at least 216,000 tons of shipping.

During the night of 22–23 May 1941 the newest ship in the German fleet, the *Bismarck*, accompanied by a heavy cruiser, the *Prinz Eugen*, debouched from the Denmark Strait to join in the hunt.

The *Bismarck* deserved to be called the pride of the Kriegsmarine. She was the most powerful warship of her time with her eight 15-inch and twelve 5.9-inch guns and her thirty-two 4.1-inch and 37mm anti-aircraft weapons. Her formidable armour was responsible for nearly 15,000 tons of her total displacement of 35,000 tons.

Spotted by the *Norfolk*, the two German warships were intercepted at dawn between Ireland

GERMAN NAVY II

1. Rear-Admiral in full dress—2. Ensign 1st Class in full service dress (formal undress) with frock coat—3. Captain in full service dress (formal undress) with frock coat—4. Vice-Admiral in service dress—5. Surgeon-Admiral in walking-out dress—6. Rear-Admiral (Senior Administrative Official of the Naval Ministry) in formal dress (evening and gala dress) —7. Captain in full service dress (formal undress) with frock coat—8. Captain in service dress—9. Commander in walking-out dress—10. Lieutenant-Commander in service dress—11. Lieutenant in full service dress (formal undress) with frock coat—12. Bandmaster in full service dress (formal undress) with frock coat—13. Chief Petty Officer of the Naval Institute in service dress—14. Machinist in walking-out dress—15. Ensign in service dress—16. Ensign 1st Class in service dress—17. Petty Officer in summer full dress—18. Machinist 3rd Class in summer full dress

and Greenland on 24 May by the battlecruiser *Hood* and the battleship *Prince of Wales*, both British. Battle was joined at a range of between six and seven miles. Five minutes later the *Bismarck*'s third salvo sent the *Hood* to the bottom after having caused an explosion in her magazines. Lightly damaged but deprived of the use of her ten 14-inch guns, whose installation had been faulty, the *Prince of Wales* had to retire for the time being and await reinforcements.

The *Bismarck*, herself somewhat damaged, continued on her way, knowing that she had won the biggest naval victory since the outbreak of hostilities.

The two raiders, pursued by a veritable posse of warships, raced south. During the night of 25–26 May, they managed to shake off their pursuers but the *Bismarck* was sighted at dawn by an aircraft from the *Ark Royal*. The more fortunate *Prinz Eugen* eluded all such searches.

From now on the *Bismarck* had half the Royal Navy against her. The aircraft carrier *Victorious* and the cruisers *Norfolk* and *Suffolk* among others were subsequently joined by the *Sheffield*, the *Renown*, the *Rodney* (with her 16-inch guns), the *Ramilles* and a flotilla of destroyers. Harried on all sides, she was only a few hundred miles from Brest when torpedo planes succeeded in damaging her rudder and propellers. In a hopeless position and incapable of manoeuvre, she fought to the last round just as Admiral Lütjens had vowed in a last signal. She sank with her colours flying at 10.36 on 27 May after having been hit by several scores of tons of shells. A salvo of nine torpedoes launched by the *Dorsetshire* struck her when her guns had been silenced.

The tragic adventure of the *Bismarck* sounded the death-knell for major German surface naval operations in the Atlantic.

Back at Brest after their raiding operations the *Scharnhorst* and *Gneisenau*, joined by the *Prinz Eugen*, were subjected to six months of air attacks by the RAF. Then, in February 1942, they attempted the 'Channel Dash' and were successful: in their own words, they inflicted on the British 'unprecedented humiliation'.

Even though they had got back to Germany these ships of the line had nevertheless nearly reached the end of their careers. Lying in wait along the Norwegian coastline, the *Tirpitz*, the *Admiral Scheer* and the *Admiral Hipper* achieved a last great victory over the ill-fated convoy PQ 17. In December 1943 the *Scharnhorst*, launched against another convoy, came up against a dozen enemy ships and was destroyed, taking with her into the icy Arctic waters virtually the whole of her 1,900-man crew. Eleven months later the *Tirpitz*, crushed by bombs, capsized in Tromsö Fjord.

The famous Kriegsmarine song, which says: '*Auf einem Seemansgrab, da glühen keine Rosen*' ('Roses don't bloom on a sailor's tomb'), was only too cruelly illustrated by these successive disasters.

ACTIONS IN THE MEDITERRANEAN

The attack on Taranto

Under the sunny Mediterranean skies, actions between Italy and Great Britain, the latter sometimes supported by France, were not long in coming. In fact the French demand for an armistice (17 June 1940) came too soon after Italy's entry into the war (10 June) for the Anglo-French naval forces to be able to assert their superiority, and from then onwards the Mediterranean became a closed battleground in which the British and Italians confronted each other.

Restricted to using bases in Egypt, Malta and Gibraltar alone, the British Mediterreanean Fleet

GERMAN NAVY III

1. Chief Petty Officer, coast artillery—2. Sub-Lieutenant coast artillery—3. Warrant Officer 1st Class, coast artillery—4. Seaman 2nd Class, coast artillery (harbour installation)—5–7. Seamen in walking-out dress—8. Shore parade dress—9. Landing rig—10. Seaman in short overcoat—11. Sub mariner in leather uniform—12. Submariner in khaki service uniform

Campaign badges: 13. Narvik—14. Submarines (1939)—15. Destroyer—16. Minesweeper and submarine chaser—17. Naval artillery—18. Auxiliary cruiser—19. Battleship and cruisers—20. Blockade runner—21. Torpedo boats—22. Crimea

suddenly found itself in a disquieting situation. Fortunately for the Royal Navy, the Italian fleet, which had grown too quickly, was not completely prepared for battle. The British admiral, Lord Cunningham, decided to strike at the Italian battleships, which were much more powerful than his own, in their home port. The aircraft carrier *Illustrious*, the newest of her class, laden with torpedo aircraft, was to take 6 battleships, 8 torpedo boats and 20 destroyers by surprise at their anchorage in the major port of Taranto. The attack was carried out during the night of 10–11 November and succeeded magnificently. Three battleships, the *Littorio*, the *Cavour* and the *Caio Dulcio*, were seriously damaged for the loss of only two aircraft. After this masterstroke Cunningham was able to support without serious hindrance the operations of British troops along the Libyan coastal plain.

The *Illustrious*, nevertheless, was destined to spend a very bad fifteen minutes on 10 January 1941 when the Stukas of the German 10th Air Corps, based on Sicily and in the Dodecanese, found her to be a target rivalling them in skill and daring. Over a span of seven hours the German pilots multiplied their attacks and managed to hit her with six 500-kg bombs, one of which struck the middle of the flight deck, killing 80 men and destroying 40 aircraft. Not without difficulty, the British took their aircraft carrier, which was in danger of being consumed by fire, into the temporary shelter of Malta, from where she was subsequently able to get back to Alexandria.

The Stukas themselves soon had Malta-based fighters at their throats, for the island proved to be the best aircraft carrier of all.

The Battle of Matapan
Known to the Italians as the Battle of Gaudo after an island to the south of Crete, this dour struggle began as a result of a sortie by the Italian Navy against the convoys bound for Greece, which was launched on 26 March 1941. Split into two powerful groups, the Italians were very quickly spotted by British naval aircraft and Admiral Iachino soon became convinced of the utter futility of an operation in which he would not have the slightest chance of meeting even the smallest enemy convoy.

Because of their misplaced sense of pride the Italian Naval High Command, the Supermarina, were anxious to impress their German allies, and ordered Iachino to continue on his mission. The Admiral obeyed, but succeeded, however, in withdrawing his forces in time after an initial inconclusive skirmish between the *Vittorio Veneto* and the British light cruisers.

Falling into line with the *Vittorio Veneto*, the British endured afresh the dangerously accurate fire of this battleship at a range of about seven and a half miles. Lord Cunningham then launched his torpedo planes and one of them, by a lucky hit,

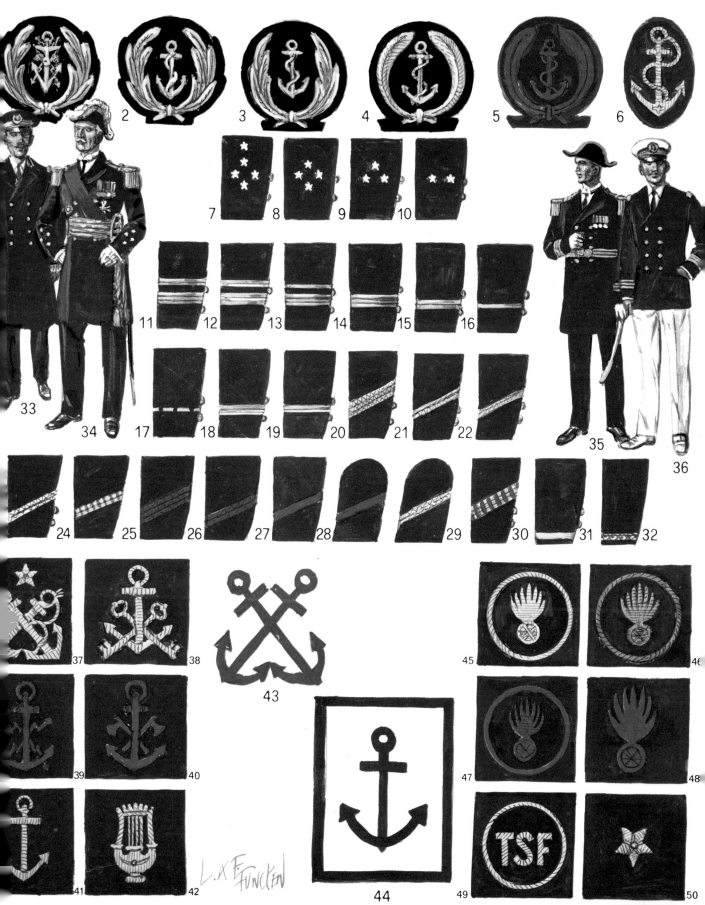

L.*F.*FUNCKEN

managed to stop this powerful ship, while another aircraft immobilised the cruiser *Pola*.

Cunningham then decided to try a night attack. It was in this that a formidable new weapon – radar[1] – was to play a part. To the amazement of the Italians the British opened fire on their cruisers, *Zara* and *Fiume*, which had come to lend a hand to the *Pola*. The two ships literally exploded at the first salvo. In the mêlée which followed between Italian torpedo boats and British destroyers the aircraft carrier *Formidable* nearly came to grief, for she was momentarily mistaken for an enemy ship by the battleship *Warspite*. Finally two Italian torpedo boats foundered and the *Pola*, the involuntary cause of this catastrophe, was sunk at dawn by a torpedo after her crew had been taken off. The Italians had lost 2,400 sailors in the first major naval battle of the Second World War.

The Reply

German airmen struck back the following month with the occupation of Greece, and again in May with their victory on Crete. There the British lost 3 cruisers and 6 destroyers while 7 ships, including 2 battleships and an aircraft carrier, were badly damaged. Six months later a 31,000-ton battleship, the *Barham*, foundered, torpedoed by the U-355. And on 18 December the cruisers based on Malta lost one of their number in a minefield while two others were seriously damaged.

But the cruellest and most spectacular blow had not yet been struck. The next day Italian frogmen blew up the battleships *Queen Elizabeth* and *Valiant* in the port of Alexandria. Eight hours earlier, in the distant China Sea, the battleship *Prince of Wales* and the battlecruiser *Repulse* had been destroyed by the Japanese.[2]

In 1942 the heavy cruiser *Manchester* and five other ships were to be sunk by the torpedoes of the formidable MAS[3] fast motor-boats.

However, the Italian fleet were lacking in fuel and could not exploit the advantage which these British losses had given it, so that it was limited to conducting a convoy war in the *rotta della morte* (course of death) – the treacherous Sicilian Strait

1 We will discuss this again in vol. 4.

2 We will discuss this again in vol. 4.

3 MAS for *motoscafi antisommergibile* (fast anti-submarine vessels).

COMPARATIVE STRENGTHS OF THE MAJOR NAVAL POWERS IN 1939

	GREAT BRITAIN	FRANCE	GERMANY	ITALY
Battleships	12 (9)	7 (4)	5 (4)	4 (4)
Battlecruisers	3	—	—	—
Heavy cruisers	15	7	2 (3)	7 (5)
Anti-aircraft cruisers	6	—	—	—
Cruisers	43 (19)	10 (3)	6 (4)	14
Aircraft-carriers	5 (6)	1 (2)	—	—
Destroyers	176 (8)	59	22 (12)	61 (30)
Torpedo-boats	26 (10)	12 (5)	12	70 (6)
Submarines	57 (18)	78 (13)	70 (?)	104 (28)
Sloops, escort vessels, etc.	52 (7)	50	10	—

The figures in brackets indicate the number of ships under construction.

FRENCH NAVY II

1. Reserve Midshipman in ordinary service dress—2. Senior Chief Petty Officer in ceremonial dress—3. Chief Petty Officer in No. 2 dress (No. 1 dress had epaulettes added: see fig. 2)—4. Petty Officer 1st Class wearing greatcoat—5. Petty Officer 2nd Class of the Petty Officers' cadre—6. Petty Officer 3rd Class in tropical dress—7. Petty Officer 1st Class in landing rig—8. Petty Officer 2nd Class in landing rig— 9. Non-specialist Seaman (Ordinary Seaman)—10. As abov in summer uniform—11. Seaman 3rd Class, provision certificate, in blue flannel jersey—12. Seaman 3rd Class i tropical dress—13. Yeoman in tropical dress—14. Seama 2nd Class in denim jersey—15. Seaman 1st Class in deni jersey—16. Seaman 2nd Class in blue flannel jersey with th denim jersey on top—17. Seaman 1st Class wearing the tw types of jersey together—18. Seaman 2nd Class wearing th tropical short-sleeved vest

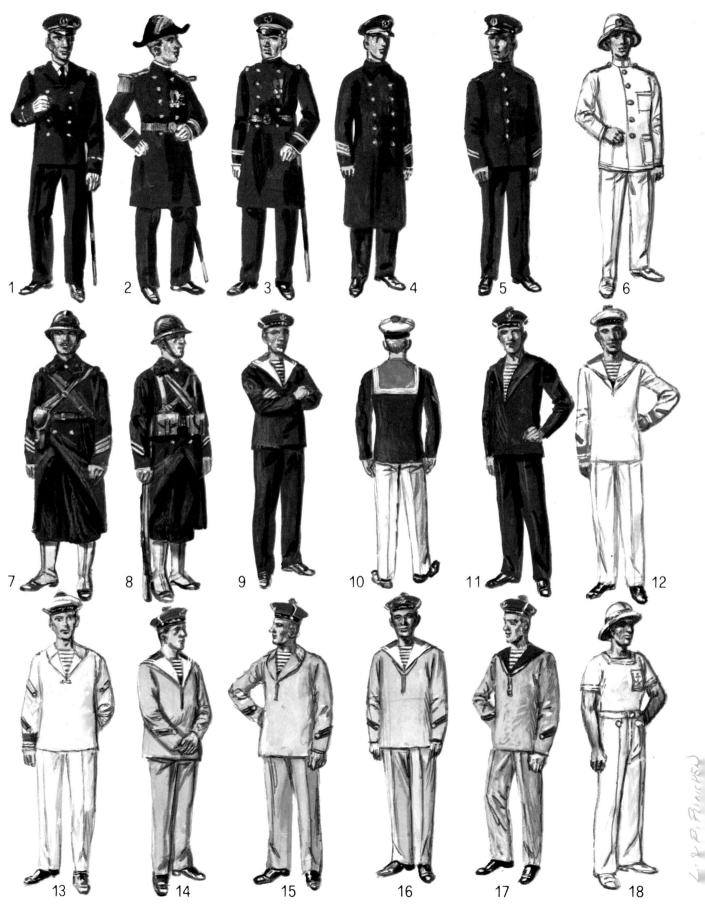

through which the Axis forces in North Africa were supplied.

THE ROYAL NAVY

Legend has it that the bow of black ribbon that adorns the caps of the sailors of the Royal Navy is worn as a mark of respect to commemorate the death of Nelson. This is quite untrue, as is the claim that the three blue stripes on the collar symbolise the three great naval victories won by this national hero: this number was fixed for no precise reason when the dress regulations were elaborated in 1857.

Since 1914–1918 very few changes have been made to the uniforms of the Royal Navy, so that the reader will be able to work them out for himself by comparing the illustrations in this volume with those in the second volume of *Arms and Uniforms of The First World War*. Only one modification need be noted. In 1941, as a result of difficulties in obtaining supplies of gold braid, officers commissioned from this time on wore their rank insignia on half the sleeve only and not all around it as previously.

Officers had the right to wear seven different forms of dress. Here we will mention only three that were not in fact worn in wartime: the full dress uniform, with the two-pointed cocked ceremonial hat, and the mess and ball dress.

The supreme head of the Royal Navy was the King himself and the abbreviation HMS (His Majesty's Ship), which preceded the name of each ship, was not just a meaningless formula. The Sovereign entrusted the administration of his navy to the Board of the Admiralty, which embraced a whole hierarchy of important officials, ranging from the First Lord to the Rear Admiral of the United Kingdom and including the 1st, 2nd, 3rd, 4th and 5th Sea Lords, etc.

In 1939 the effective manpower of the Royal Navy amounted to 133,000. This figure was only slightly lower than those of the preceding periods: 146,000 in 1941 and 145,000 during the Napoleonic Wars.

THE ROYAL MARINES

Nicknamed the 'Jollies', the Royal Marines represent one of the most famous bodies of men of all the world's fighting forces. Their foundation goes back to 1664 – when they were known as the 'Lord High Admiral's Regiment' – and they have never ceased to distinguish themselves throughout the succeeding centuries. The laurel wreath which today adorns their flag and their badge was granted to them in 1761 after the siege of Belle Isle. The title of 'Royal Marines' was bestowed upon them in 1802 and the globe and Royal Monogram on their badge followed in 1827.

Under the motto *Per mare per terram* (By sea, by land), the 'Jollies' served with distinction during the Second World War. They saw action in Crete and in Norway; on the *Repulse* and *Prince of Wales*; at Singapore, in the actions against the *Bismarck* and the *Scharnhorst*; at Dieppe, in Sicily and finally in Normandy, right up to the final battle.

Over the years certain British regiments have served as marines, but they should not be confused with the genuine Royal Marines, who retain the right to remain seated for the Loyal Toast and to march with fixed bayonets through the streets of London. In Great Britain tradition is not an empty word.

THE FRENCH NAVY

Under the stimulus of the Navy Minister, Georges Leygues, France endowed herself between 1925

FRENCH NAVY III

1. Seaman 3rd Class in tropical cotton vest—2. Seaman 2nd Class in blue serge jumper—3. Seaman 1st Class in greatcoat—4. Armed Seaman, graduate of Petty Officer school—5. As above, in summer uniform—6. As above, in winter uniform—7. Same, back view—8-9. Seaman 3rd Class of the battalion of Fusiliers Marins in parade dress—10. Seaman 3rd Class in landing rig—11. Same, back view—12. Seaman in waterproof coat (raincoat) for walking-out dress—13. Seaman in greatcoat as worn on watch—14. Seaman in sou'wester and oilskins—15. Seaman dressed for very cold climates—16. Special dress for crew members of high-speed craft—17. Submariners' dress—18. Hooded cloak, worn with walking-out dress by Mechanical Engineering Apprentice and Apprentice Mechanician

1   2   3   4   5   6

7   8   9   10   11   12

13   14   15   16   17   18

and 1939 with a splendid fleet – the finest she had ever possessed. This was all made possible by the tireless and brilliant work of such admirals as Violette, Duran-Vieil and Darlan.

The outbreak of war in 1939 found the French Navy in the middle of a period of expansion. It was a force whose worth was fully recognised by its British allies. However, a strange fate was to overwhelm this fine fleet which, after a few initial exploits against submarines, was to be afflicted by a long series of painful sacrifices.

It was in the hell of Dunkirk that the *Sirocco*, the *Adroit*, the *Chacal* and a large number of other ships were lost. Then came the French capitulation, the British ultimatum over Mers-el-Kebir and the slaughter of 1,300 French sailors by their former allies.[1] Finally, on 27 November 1942, the fleet at Toulon was scuttled to prevent it from falling into German hands after the latter had invaded the so-called 'Free Zone' of France.[2]

This drama opened the way for the French naval units based in North Africa to go over to the side of the Allies, where they rejoined the handful of sailors who, since 1940, had thrown in their lot with Great Britain and served under the name of the 'Free French Naval Forces'.

THE GERMAN NAVY

The main architect of Germany's naval regeneration was incontestably Grand Admiral Erich Raeder, but this brilliantly able officer's plans were undermined by Adolf Hitler's obstinacy and total lack of comprehension. When war was declared the Kriegsmarine was still so far from being ready to confront the Allied fleets that, according to the Grand Admiral, it would be good only for showing the world how to die bravely!

Raeder had submitted to the Führer his Plan Z, which should have given Germany the fleet she needed. If Germany had adopted this plan, she would have had at her disposal some 13 battleships, 33 cruisers, 4 aircraft carriers and 250 submarines, but not before 1948.

It was with infinitely smaller forces than this that the Third Reich actually entered the war at

sea, with the unsatisfactory results which have already been described. Even Admiral Dönitz's pack of submarines, for all its spirit of aggression, was not enough to snatch victory by itself.

THE ITALIAN NAVY

Classed as the fifth naval power, Italy entered the war in June 1940 with forces which suffered from a disastrous lack of preparation. Taking the fuel needed by the fleet as a case in point, after only nine months the stocks had fallen to 600,000 tons, and were further reduced to 60,000 in 1942. This chronic state of affairs, coupled with a total lack of any strategic doctrine, hampered the proper exploitation of this magnificent fleet, which was endowed with excellent ships manned by brave and skilful crews. Badly supported by an air force based on Mussolini's vision of Italy as the gigantic unsinkable aircraft-carrier, the *Regia Marina* could only shine in individual actions. A number of admirals were to die with their colours flying, like the great Carlo Berganini who was killed on the *Roma*; others, even less fortunate, such as Inigo Campioni and Luigi Mascherpa, were shot by a firing squad following the Italian surrender.

---

1 On 3 July 1940 the British called upon the squadron anchored in the roadstead of Mers-el-Kebir, off the coast of Algeria, either to join them or to let themselves be disarmed. The French admiral refused both proposals and the British opened fire.
2 9 cruisers, 1 seaplane tender, 25 destroyers and 25 submarines

FRENCH NAVY IV

1–2. Naval airmen in summer and winter flying clothing—3. Naval bandsman (Seaman 3rd Class: musician)—4. Seaman on attached duty with a Harbour Pilot—5. Maritime Gendarmerie

Special Headgear: 6. Anti-flash or blast helmet worn by naval gunners—7. Helmet worn by crews of high-speed craft—8. Flying helmet—9. Tropical flying helmet—10. Colonial or tropical helmet worn by naval officers, and Seamen 1st 2nd and 3rd Class—11. Prisoner's cap

12. Calf-length boot with wooden sole and rubber uppers—13. Rubber ankle boot with wooden sole—14. Wooden-soled boot

Breast badges: Air Branch 15. Pilot (Naval Air Arm)—16. Air Mechanics, Radio Operators, Air Gunner-bombardiers and Observers (aircrew)—17. Dirigible (or airship) Pilot—18. Captive balloon observers

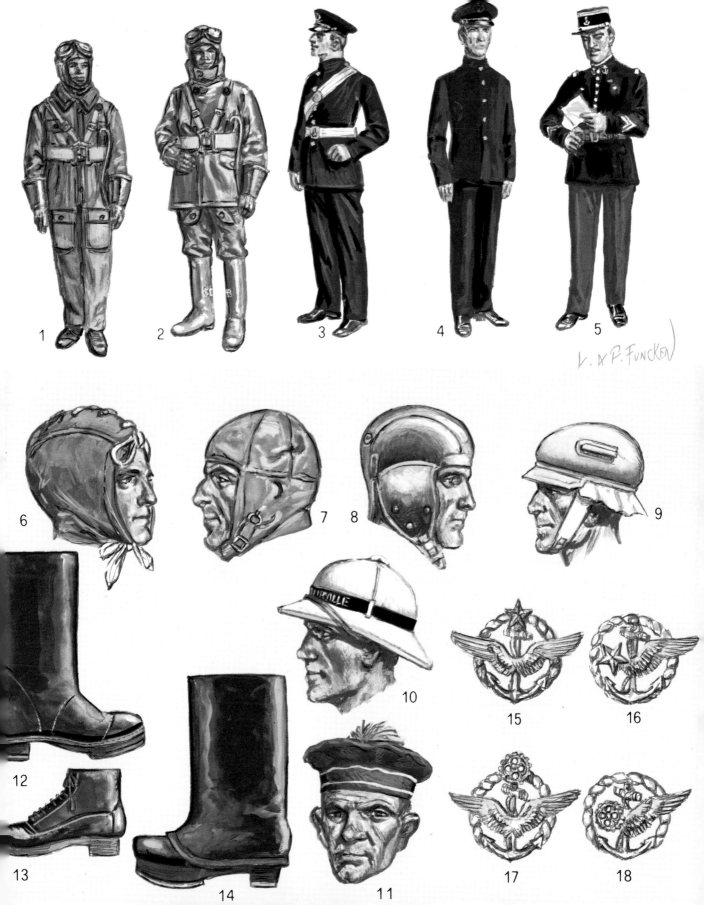

1   2   3   4   5

L. & P. Funcken

6   7   8   9

10   15   16

12

13   14   11   17   18

THE POLISH NAVY[1]

We have mentioned the first naval action of the Second World War, in which the tiny Polish fleet faced the joint might of the Luftwaffe and the German Baltic Fleet.

On 1st September 1939 the sloop *Mazur* became the first victim of the enemy bombers and sank in the port of Gdynia, although she continued to fire at her assailants until her guns disappeared beneath the surface. Other units of this fragment of the Polish fleet managed to find refuge in the port of Hela after a chase lasting two days. On the following day two German torpedo-boats closed with the intention of finishing off the already badly damaged ships but, to their great surprise, they met with such a violent response that they were forced to withdraw hastily. One of the torpedo-boats sank before reaching Danzig. However, this respite did not last for long and a few hours after their unexpected victory the minelayer *Gryf*, the minesweeper *Mewa* and the torpedo-boat *Wicher* were destroyed by aircraft.

The larger Polish naval units had fortunately put to sea as early as 30 August and were already in British waters when the drama at Hela was being enacted. There remained the five submarines which were cruising off Gdynia or in the Gulf of Puck, but these too managed to get to Britain in spite of the pursuit mounted against them.

The Polish fleet was therefore able to serve the Allied cause. Reinforced by the cruiser *Dragon*, which was lent by the Royal Navy, it fought throughout the war with an ardour worthy of a people with such an heroic past.

THE NORWEGIAN NAVY

Compared with the army, the Norwegian navy appeared to be fairly impressive, since it comprised 4 battleships, 7 destroyers, 7 torpedo-boats, 9 patrol boats, 2 minelayers and 5 submarines. Admittedly only the submarines and some of the destroyers were reasonably modern.

Paralysed by the suddenness of the German attack, the 2,000 Norwegian sailors could offer

only token resistance. Thus the *Norge* and her twin-sister ship, the *Eidsvoll*, were sunk in a few seconds; the latter barely had time to point her guns towards the enemy. Few ships managed to escape from the trap; only the destroyer *Sleipner* and the submarine B1 reached the Allied camp.

THE FINNISH NAVY

With a mere 4,000 sailors and few warships Finland could play only an extremely minor role in the naval operations of the Second World War. Two 3,900-ton coastal defence vessels, 4 gunboats, 5 submarines and a handful of motor-boats and minelayers represented the sum total of the Finnish naval forces.

ROYAL NAVY

1. Admiral of the Fleet—2. Admiral—3. Vice-Admiral—4. Rear-Admiral. The epaulette bearing an anchor and two stars, when accompanied by the same rings, denotes the rank of Commodore 1st Class—5. Commodore 2nd Class—6. Captain—7. Commander—8. Lieutenant-Commander—9. Lieutenant—10. Sub-Lieutenant—11. Warrant Officer—12. Peaked cap of an Admiral—13. Peak of a Commodore's cap—14. Officers: a. Officers' cap badge; b. Petty Officers' cap badge—15-16. Lieutenant and Paymaster-Lieutenant of the Royal Naval Reserve—17-18. Lieutenant and Surgeon-Lieutenant of the Royal Naval Volunteer Reserve (the latter should have a red stripe between the two gold stripes)

Various branches of the Royal Navy: (the rank shown in illustrations 19-27 is that of Commander)—19. Air Branch (Fleet Air Arm)—20. Engineer—21. Surgeon—22. Dental—23. Accountant (Paymaster)—24. Instructor—25. Shipwright and Constructor—26. Ordnance—27. Electrical engineer—28. HM Coast Guards: cap badges of Officers and Petty Officers—29. Chief Inspector—30. Deputy Chief Inspector—31. Inspector—32. District Officer—33. Station Officer—34. Cap and badge of the Royal Marines—35. Colonel—36. Lieutenant-Colonel—37. Major—38. Captain—39. Lieutenant—40 Second Lieutenant

Rank, proficiency and trade badges (worn on the left sleeve): 41. Petty Officer—42. Leading Seaman—As above, but worn on the right sleeve: 43. Gunner's Mate—44. Captain of Gun 1st Class—45. Torpedo Gunner's Mate—46. Range-taker 1st Class—47. Visual Signalman, 1st Class—48. Diver—49. Observer's Mate—50. Chief Photographer—51. Leading Stoker and Stoker—52. Wireless Telegraphist 1st Class—53. Submarine Detector Operator—54. Surveying Recorder—55. Physical Training Instructor 1st Class—56. Chief Armourer and Armourer—57. Regulating Petty Officer—58. Supply Rating—59. Marksman's badge (Musketry)—60. Bugler

[1] For ranks and uniforms, see vol. 1, pages 92 to 95.

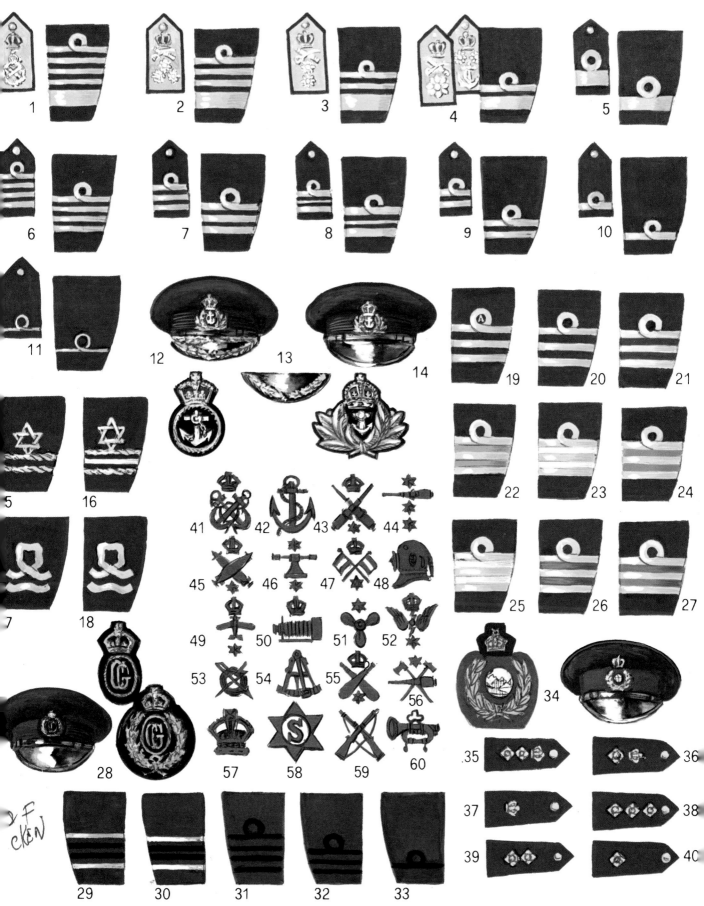

1 2 3 4 5

6 7 8 9 10

11 12 13 14

19 20 21

15 16 22 23 24

17 18 25 26 27

41 42 43 44

45 46 47 48

49 50 51 52

53 54 55 56

34

57 58 59 60

28

35 36

37 38

2 F
CKEN

29 30 31 32 33

39 40

THE BELGIAN NAVY

On 15 September 1939 the Minister of National Defence set up a makeshift body, called the Naval Corps, with the object of protecting the Belgian coast and ensuring that the country could be supplied with food and raw materials by sea. This force was comprised of 14 officers, 18 petty officers and 512 seamen and marines.

The three flotillas were equipped with an improbable collection of pilot-boats, yachts and trawlers. All had been requisitioned, with the exception of the yacht *Prince Charles*, which had been offered by a patriotic yachtsman.

As the threat from Germany became more obvious, the Naval Corps had to abandon the Belgian coast after having scuttled those ships which were no longer seaworthy. A perilous voyage took this ill-fated armada close to Bordeaux and then on to Spain where they were interned. Only one vessel was able to reach Portugal and, from there, to struggle to England.

Uniforms

The navy-blue uniforms had been determined by a ministerial despatch of 29 March 1939.

Some of the features of the dress worn by officers were as follows:

> The peaked cap followed the army pattern, with a fouled and crowned anchor beneath the national cockade on the head-band; the chinstrap was a double gold band and the peak was in black leather.
> The double-breasted jacket had two rows of five buttons, was adorned with two epaulette loops and provided with two large pockets with rectangular flaps; the trousers were slightly flared.
> The greatcoat also followed the army pattern with gold epaulette loops.

The jacket and greatcoat bore rank insignia in the same way as in the army on dark-blue velvet patches. On the peaked cap the gold stripes ran right around the cap-band, after the fashion of the French Navy.

Colonel: 5 lines of gold braid
Lieutenant-Colonel: 5 lines of braid: 4 in gold, the centre one in silver
Major: 4 lines of gold braid
Captain-Major: 3 lines of gold braid
Captain: 3 lines of braid: 2 in gold, the middle one in silver
Lieutenant: 2 lines of gold braid
Second (or Sub-) Lieutenant: 1 line of gold braid

It should be noted that there were in fact no Colonels or Lieutenant-Colonels in the Corps.

The petty officers wore the same jacket and peaked cap as the officers. The chin-strap for Chief Petty Officers was a double silver cord or band and was in black leather for the other petty officers. All had a silver stripe running round the cap-band.

The rank of Chief Petty Officer was indicated by a silver star at the end of the sleeves, and the other ranks by stripes known as 'sardines' in gilt braid.

Petty Officer 1st Class: 3 lines of gold braid
Petty Officer 2nd Class: 2 lines of gold braid
Petty Officer 3rd Class: 1 line of gold braid

ITALIAN NAVY

1. Admiral of the Fleet—2. Admiral—3. Shoulder boards worn by Admirals (left) and Senior Officers (i.e. Captains to Ranking Lieutenants)—4. Vice-Admiral—5. Rear-Admiral (Upper Half)—6. Rear-Admiral—7. Captain—8. Commander—9. Lieutenant-Commander—10. Lieutenant—11. Sub-Lieutenant—12. Ensign—13. Petty Officer (Upper Half): Medical Branch—14. Petty Officer (Lower Half): Gunner—15. Chief Petty Officer 1st Class (worn on white uniform)—16. Chief Petty Officer 2nd Class (worn across the shoulder on the blue uniform)—17. Chief Petty Officer 3rd Class—18. Leading Seaman—19. Seaman 1st Class, Signalman—20. Seaman 2nd Class, Gunner. The red stripes denote the 1st, 2nd, 3rd or 4th squadron.

Speciality insignia: 21. Ordnance Repairman—22. Machinist—23. Gunlayer—24. Fire Controlman—25. Damage Controlman or Fireman—26. Bugler

27. Gunner in combat dress—28. Lieutenant in service dress—29. Chief Petty Officer 2nd Class in summer dress. The same uniform, in beige linen, was worn in the tropics—30. Leading Seaman in service dress. In summer, the white jersey was worn with white or navy blue trousers

31. The *Conte di Cavour*—32. The *Garibaldi*—33. The *Bolzano*—34. The *Andrea Doria*

As the illustration shows, Seamen 1st, 2nd and 3rd Class wore a uniform almost identical to that of the French Navy. The French-type beret, however, had a sky-blue pompom and the ribbon ended in two tails, 15cm in length, which hung down over the neck. The ribbon initially bore the Flemish title *Marine Korps* in gold letters on the front, but this inscription was too similar to the German *Deutsches Marinekorps* so, in February 1940, it was replaced by the simple word *Marine* which had the added advantage of cutting short the linguistic dispute between French and Dutch-speaking elements.[1]

Numerous Belgian sailors found refuge in Britain and managed, though not without some difficulties, to create a national section within the Royal Navy. Accepted with some reservations, the Belgians earned the admiration of their allies, however difficult they were to impress. In the end they won the right to serve under the Belgian flag on board two warships lent by the Royal Navy.

The French and British Naval Air Arms

From the very beginnings of the conquest of the air sailors became passionately interested in aeronautics, and some of them have earned a special niche in the history of aviation as well as a place in naval history.

In France well before 1900 Commander du Temple invented an aluminium flying machine with a retractable undercarriage which flew in the form of a scaled-down model only, because of lack of funds. It is to this great engineer that we also owe the multi-tubed boiler, which was destined to have a brilliant future.

At the beginning of the First World War the French naval air arm had only 8 seaplanes. However, the need for convoy protection became a vital task and led the Government to establish the naval air bases of Le Havre, Boulogne, Toulon, Bizerta and La Pallice. In 1916 159 seaplanes were actively participating in the struggle above the oceans. One of these naval airmen, Paul-Marcel Teste,[2] later became the advocate and initiator of ship-borne aviation. In this he showed an energy and boldness remarkable at a time when the general euphoria led people to neglect the very means which were necessary to safeguard the peace.

Commander Teste, who died prematurely, did not see the almost total ruin of all his efforts when, in 1939, the squadrons of the aircraft-carrier *Béarn* were disembarked and based on land with their obsolete aircraft.

The naval pilots nevertheless did their duty splendidly and brought down scores of German aircraft, not, however, without suffering heavy losses in their attempt to stem the tide.

After the defeat many naval airmen escaped to the 'free world'. In Great Britain they formed the mixed naval and air force fighter group 'Ile-de-France' in 1941 and, a little later, the reconnaissance group 6FE whose forgotten heroes watched over the transport ships, which were stalked by enemy submarines. Even if they lacked the

1 The content of this chapter is drawn entirely from a study by the sadly-missed Chief Curator of the Musée de l'Armée in Brussels. Monsieur Louis Lecomte, which appeared in 'Le Carnet de la Fourragère', No. 8 in 1951.
2 Born in Lorient in 1892, he died at Villacoublay in 1925.

FINNISH, NORWEGIAN AND BELGIAN NAVIES

Finnish Navy: 1. Admiral—2. Vice-Admiral—3. Rear-Admiral—4. Captain—5. Commander—6. Lieutenant-Commander—7. Lieutenant—8. Sub-Lieutenant—9. Ensign—10. Reserve Ensign—11. Petty Officer 1st Class (Machinist)—12. Petty Officer 2nd and 3rd Class (Torpedoman)—13. Petty Officer 4th Class (Signalman)—14. Leading Seaman—15. Sergeant-Major—16. Sergeant—17. Seaman 1st Class

Norwegian Navy: 18. Admiral—19. Vice-Admiral—20. Rear Admiral—21. Commodore—22. Captain—23. Commander—24. Lieutenant-Commander and Lieutenant—25. Sub Lieutenant

26. The *Ilmarinen* (Finland)—27. The patrol boat A4 of the Belgian Naval Corps (Corps de marine)—28. The *Norg* (Norway)

29. Belgian seaman

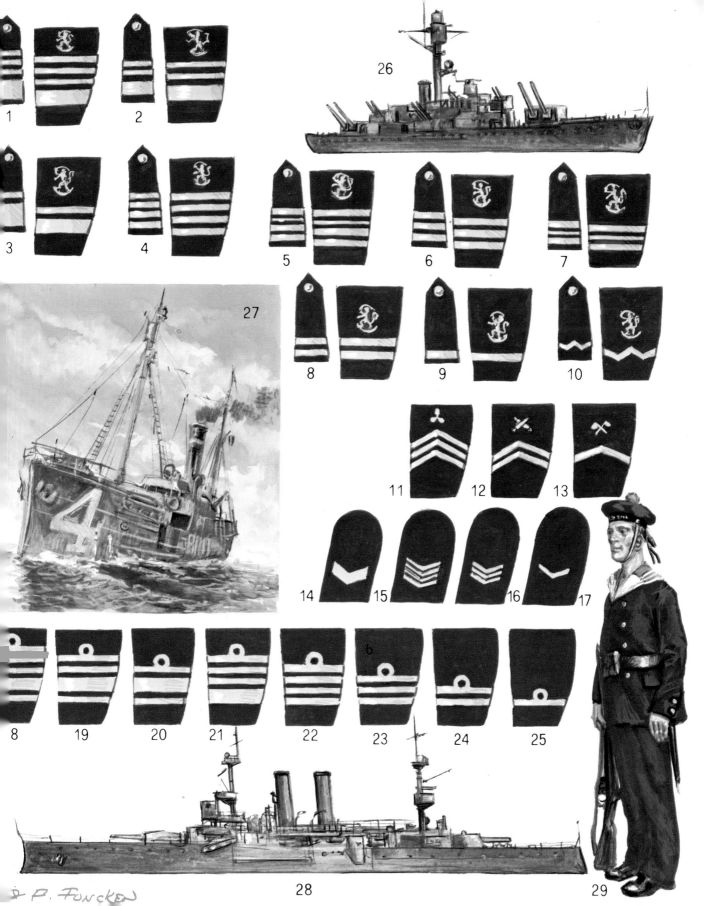

1

2

3

4

5

6

7

8

9

10

11

12

13

14

15

16

17

8

19

20

21

22

23

24

25

26

27

28

29

P. FONCKEN

panache of the fighter pilots these workers for victory nevertheless deserve our recognition.

In Britain aircraft-carriers appeared as early as the end of the 1914–1918 War. The first of these was the *Argus*, an Italian liner, which was converted for its new role in the course of construction. However, the first complete aircraft-carrier, built from scratch from the drawing-board up, was the *Hermes*. The *Furious*, of which there were five or six successive versions between 1917 and 1932, should also be mentioned. In the course of her construction this light battlecruiser was first fitted with a take-off platform on her bow section and then, in 1918, with a second platform at the stern. Finally, completely re-built between 1921 and 1925, she was given an uninterrupted flight-deck – a characteristic feature of modern aircraft-carriers. The *Furious*, the product of laborious development, was destined, nevertheless, to serve throughout the Second World War.

Thanks to improvements in engine power and performance in the sphere of carrier-borne types, the British passed from the Sopwith Cuckoo torpedo plane to the Fairey Swordfish which followed the torpedo-spotting-reconnaissance formula that was adopted in 1930.

In 1940–41 the Fairey Albacore appeared, a type similar to the Swordfish but faster. The Blackburn Skua dive-bomber – or its improved version, the Roc – could, once it had released its bomb, transform itself into a fighter to protect the slow Swordfish aircraft which launched their torpedoes from long range in level flight. There were also several carrier-borne fighter types, such as the Fairey Fulmar, the Sea Gladiator, the Sea Hurricane and the Supermarine Seafire, these last two being the naval versions of the Hurricane and Spitfire.

The British Fleet Air Arm won fame in Norway in 1940. It also took part in the sad affair at Mers-el-Kebir, but found a more glorious role in the attack on the Italian fleet at Taranto.

We will follow the development of naval aviation and describe the naval air arms of other countries in the last of the four volumes devoted to the arms and uniforms of the 1939–45 War.

FRENCH AND BRITISH NAVAL AIR ARMS

1. The aircraft-carrier *Béarn*—2. Vought V.156 of the French Navy (1939–1940)—3. Bréguet BR.521 *Bizerte* (France 1937)—4. Blackburn Roc (Great Britain 1940)—5. Fairey Albacore (Great Britain 1940)—6. The British aircraft carrier *Hermes* (sunk in 1942 by a Japanese aircraft)

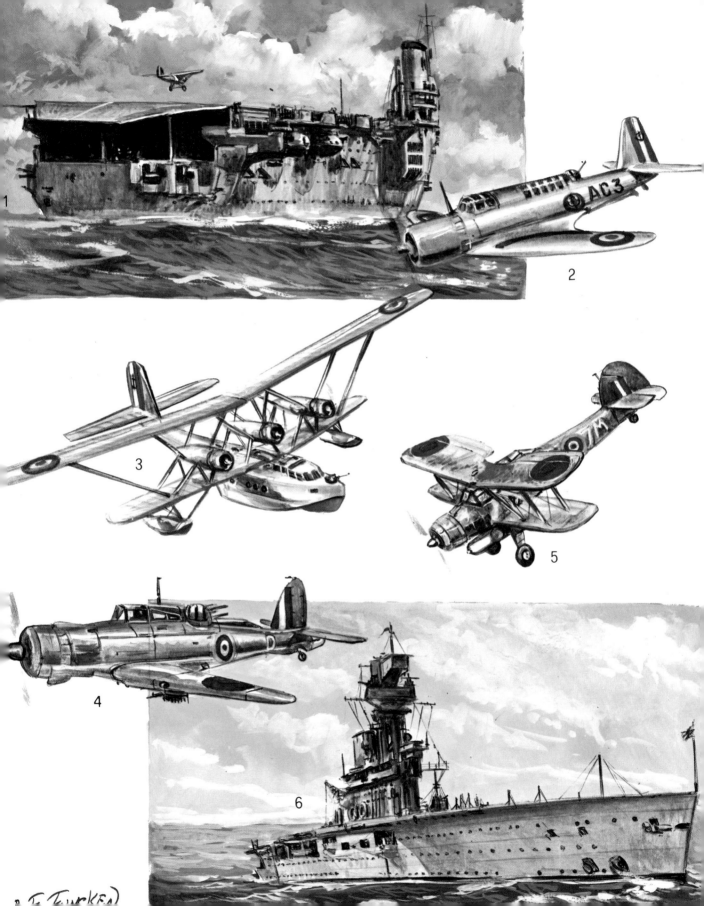

1

2

3

5

4

6

PART FIVE

THE WORLD AT WAR

THE UNITED STATES

The American Army

From 1930 onwards the United States began to react defensively to the series of Nazi and Fascist victories and their increasingly aggressive stance. The government had laid the foundation for the mobilisation of industry, and now in 1937 General Malin Craig, chief of staff of the army, was put in charge of the preparations for civilian mobilisation, under a plan in which the army and the National Guard would combine to make up a force some 400,000 strong.

The National Guard was manned by volunteers from every class of society who gave some of their time each week to military training – a system older than the United States itself. The first National Guard units were militia set up by the Boston authorities in 1636. Each state of the republic had its own National Guard until 1933, when the National Guard of the United States came into being. Though outwardly similar, it differed in that it could be called up at any time by the President of the United States without his having to refer to individual governors. Between September 1940 and October 1941 this National Guard had reached a strength of 300,000 men.

President Roosevelt and his advisers were fully aware of the dangers that threatened American sovereignty and in particular the Panama Canal Zone, which was the cornerstone of their naval defence policy. In order to strengthen the army the Rainbow Plan was put into operation.

In 1939 there were 462,000 men in the ranks, and only a few of these took part in the first large-scale exercise ever conducted on American soil. The dazzling German victories in 1939 and 1940 made it only too clear that far more severe measures were called for. Under a plan to enlarge the army still further the Selected Service and Training Bill of 16 September 1940 was the first to make provision for a civilian call-up. The result was that the army doubled in size in the space of a few months, so that by the following year it consisted of some 1,500,000 troops.

At the same time a special General Staff was created to deal with this sudden influx, to organise and train it, and the army began to expand with new armoured, anti-tank, and anti-aircraft corps. Thanks to hard work, by the autumn of 1941 the USA had 27 infantry divisions, 2 cavalry divisions,

AMERICAN ARMY I

1. 1944 Infantryman wearing 1943 model fatigue dress adapted as summer battledress. He is armed with a Thompson M1 machine-gun and a 1911 model A1 pistol. The coiled flex hanging from the holster was tied in Western fashion round the thigh—2. Machine-gunner in greatcoat armed with 1917 Browning model A1 30 calibre (7.6mm) machine-gun. There was also a 50 calibre (12.7mm) version called the HB M2 Garand—3 3rd division infantryman with Garand M1 rifle.—4. 'The Red Diamond' division captain in 1945, wearing winter dress with ranking marked on his helmet cover, brandishing the M1 carbine—5. Infantryman in winter dress and white helmet cover. As with other armies, white over-garments could be worn on open snowy ground—6. Infantryman in summer battledress worn with shirt only; he is firing the 1917 model 7.62mm Enfield rifle. The brown chin straps over the helmet visor (figs 1–6) are part of the pressed fibre helmet lining, while the wide chin straps, often worn loose, are part of the steel helmets.

Insignia worn on sleeves: 7. 1st division—8. 2nd 'Indian Head' division—9. 4th division—10. 7th division—11. 8th division—12. 24th division—13. 25th division.

5 armoured divisions and 35 air force divisions.

One might have expected that after Pearl Harbour America would consider Japan as her main enemy, but in fact – and this was despite violent disagreement from some in high places – it was against Germany that most effort was directed. Both British and American leaders realised how important it was to set up a second front before a victory in Russia and the supply of men and materials from the conquered nations of Europe could transform Hitler into a well-nigh invincible enemy.

This was the reason behind the transfer of American troops in January 1942 to Ireland, where, although they had already been thoroughly drilled, they now underwent intensive training to put them and keep them in good shape.

Such was the flood-tide of men and materials across the Atlantic that soon most were transferred to Great Britain, and in October 1942 the first American contingents left to fight in North Africa, only to return after the elimination of the Axis forces to prepare for the great landings of June 1944. The GIs,[1] as they called themselves, took part in intensive combined land-sea exercises with British troops, and it goes without saying that the US Navy had no small role to play in the vital task of protecting the convoys that carried this mass of men and materials from the U-boat threat.

It was the dangerous lot of the two British ocean liners, the *Queen Elizabeth* and the *Queen Mary*, to carry the larger part of the US army to Europe. On one trip alone the *Queen Elizabeth* managed to bring some 15,028 men safely to port.

By the end, a staggering total of 11,260,000 soldiers had taken part in the war, excluding the navy. Losses (again excluding the navy[2]) amounted to 234,874 killed outright and 83,400 fatally wounded.

UNIFORMS

For the first months of the war the GI's uniform was very similar to that worn by the American Expeditionary Corps in the First World War.[3] Of course, the stand-up collar, a feature common to most uniforms of the period, was replaced by a soft open collar revealing shirt and tie, and puttees gave way to gaiters or stiff canvas leggings, but these minor changes hardly made the battledress more practical.

They still wore a British-style helmet and, for a relatively brief period, the awkward boy-scout style hat. The tin hat was soon replaced by a new and better helmet, the MI, based originally on a German design which entered mass production and became standard issue from 9 June 1941. It was worn over a compressed fibre helmet, slightly smaller in size, which acted as a lining or could be used on its own behind the front lines.

In 1941 the only field service dress in existence was a short dark-olive waterproof jacket. Faced with a huge army which would have to fight on many fronts and in conditions that needed special clothing, the Ordnance Corps hastened to fill the gaps that appeared in the range of uniforms available.

1 GI: the initials of Government Issue or, according to some, General Issue.
2 See the chapter on the American navy in vol. 4 for exact figures.
3 See vol. 1 of *Arms and Uniforms of the First World War*.

AMERICAN ARMY II

1. Corporal in the uniform worn in Northern Ireland and Great Britain in 1942—2. Company Sergeant-Major with new 1942–1945 uniform; as high ranking non-commissioned officers, Company Sergeant-Majors and Adjutants wore the special badge (fig. 10) instead of the arm's badge—3. A non-commissioned officer in summer walking-out dress; on his right collar he is wearing the badge shown in fig. 11, and on the left the badge shown in fig. 12, to indicate that he is seconded or on a special mission.
4. Company Sergeant-Major's cap and badge—5. Company Sergeant-Major's epaulette—6. Adjutant's epaulette—7. Non-commissioned officer's and soldier's cap—8. Cap badge, fig. 7—9. High ranking non-commissioned officer's collar badge—10. Lapel badge—11. Non-commissioned officer's and soldier's collar badge, worn on the right—12. Non-commissioned officer's and soldier's collar badge when seconded or on special duties, worn on the left—13. Wounded man's chevrons (two shown) on the right sleeve with, below, one line of braid for 3 years' service—14. 1914–18 campaign chevron, worn on the left sleeve.
Rank insignia (worn on both arms): 15. Private 1st Class—16. Corporal—17. Technician 5th Class—18. Technician 4th Class—19. Sergeant—20. Technician 3rd Class—21. Staff Sergeant—22. Technical Staff-Sergeant—23. First Sergeant—24. Master Sergeant. These last two ranks are the equivalent of Company Sergeant-Major and Adjutant (of a battalion)

A special department was set up to create the GI's new wardrobe. Spurred on by patriotism and with the help of vast numbers of advisers drawn from universities and laboratories, they succeeded in turning the GI into the best and most carefully dressed soldier in the world.

Without going so far as to enumerate all the modifications that occurred when stocks ran out and were replaced, or when minor defects came to light in the heat of battle, five major patterns of uniform stand out: service dress, and the field service dress of the years 1941, 42, 43 and 45 respectively. Of course this list excludes special-purpose uniforms.

In 1943 high boots and leather spats that tied round the ankles replaced leggings. These were made of leather worn with the smooth side next to the skin which gave this 1943 model an unusually coarse appearance. By the end of the war the army as a whole was issued with a new type of fully lacing parachute-style boot that came up to the ankle.

The officers' field service dress was identical to other ranks. In full and service dress the most significant differences were in quality and particularly in the varying shades of khaki.

The main types of battledress mentioned above and shown in the illustrations were often worn together in various combinations. Perhaps the only generalisation one can make was that the windcheater jacket with its brown knitted collar tended to be discarded in favour of the 1943 model waterproof canvas jacket. The greatcoat was worn only in very cold weather and, to judge by photographs, as little as possible even then.

THE GI IN COMBAT

Young American soldiers with no first-hand experience were thrown into battle on one front or another against a seasoned enemy, who were ready to take merciless advantage of their slightest mistake. It is from the operations after the Normandy landings that we get the clearest picture of their violent initiation. The drama of D-Day[1] itself has tended to overshadow the weeks of fighting that followed, which many people dismiss as a mere formality.

Between 6 June and 11 September the Allies lost 225,000 men, killed or wounded. The 90th division alone lost 2,000 men in five days for the gain of as many miles.

The 2nd battalion of the 120th Infantry regiment were surrounded at Mortain east of Avranches and held out for five days in one of the most heroic actions of the war in Europe.

There follows a list of infantry divisions whose insignia are illustrated with a brief description of their operations.

1 6 June 1944.

AMERICAN ARMY III

1. Officer in normal dress—2. Officer in summer dress. When no jacket was worn, rank was shown on the right of the collar and on the left arm. With the tunic as in fig. 1, rank was worn on the epaulettes—3. 1938 model forage cap. From 1933 to 1939 only the armoured corps, mechanised units and the air force wore forage caps. The illustration shows a General's cap with one star on a black velvet ground—4. A new model forage cap, eventually worn throughout the army. This is with a General's gold piping; Subalterns had gold and black piping, and Sergeant-Majors silver and black piping—5. Officer's peaked cap—6. Cap badge (fig. 5)—7. Collar and lapel badges (illustrated, the crossed rifles of the infantry)

Epaulettes: 8. General—9. Lieutenant-General—10. Major-General—11. Brigadier-General—12. Colonel—13. Lieutenant-Colonel—14. Major—15. Captain—16. 1st Lieutenant—17. 2nd Lieutenant.

Lapel insignia: 18. General administration—19. General Aide-de-Camp—20. Lieutenant-General's A.D.C.—21 Major-General's A.D.C.—22. Brigadier General's A.D.C.—23. Special badge for officers who had been attached for a least a year to the General Staff, worn on the upper right pocket (see fig. 1)—24. Staff officer—25. Officer of the National Guard—26. Military lawyer—27. Armaments—28. Field artillery—29. Tanks—30. Cavalry—31. Special service—32. Commissariat—33. Military police—34. Anti-tank corps—35. Engineers—36. Information—37. Music—38. Treasury—39. Christian chaplain—40. Inspectorate—41. Chemical warfare—42. Coastal artillery—43. Signals—44. Jewish chaplain—45. Doctor—46. Health service administration—47-48. Badges of officers and men seconded to special duties—49-50. Officers' and soldiers' badges of the WAC, the Women's Army Corps.

1st infantry division

'The Big Red One' was the first US division to come under fire in the First World War, and in 1943 it took part in the invasion of Sicily. In 1944 they landed at Omaha beach (Calvados) and continued the advance as far as Czechoslovakia.

2nd infantry division

The most decorated US division of the First World War, the 'Indian Head' took part in the D-Day landings and ended the war in Czechoslovakia.

3rd infantry division

'We're staying put' was the motto the 'Marne' division had won in the First World War. They landed in Provence in 1944 and distinguished themselves at Colmar. They were awarded the French Croix de Guerre.

4th infantry division

The Ivy division or 'Famous Fourth' fought five campaigns in 1918, took part in the liberation of Paris in 1944 and broke through the Siegfried line in four places.

5th mechanised infantry division

The 'Red Diamonds', or 'Red Devils', crossed the Meuse in 1918 and the Rhine in 1945.

7th infantry division

The 'Bayonet' division fought in Lorraine in 1918. They occupied the Aleutian Islands in 1943 before fighting at Leyte in the Philippines, at Kwajalein in the Marshall Islands and on the Ryukyu Islands off Japan.

8th infantry division

Called the 'Golden Arrow' or 'Pathfinders' in memory of the military explorer John Frémont (1813–1890), their camp too was named after him: Camp Frémont. The 8th was set up in 1918 and arrived in France after the Armistice. In 1944 they returned to France and fought in four campaigns.

24th infantry division

The 'Victory' division, set up in 1921 in Hawaii, first came under fire at Pearl Harbour, fought in New Guinea, at Leyte and at Luzon in the Philippines.

25th infantry division

'Tropic Lightning' was set up in 1941. They landed on Guadalcanal in the Solomons and fought for 165 days without pause on the island of Luzon in 1945.

We should mention here two of the most extraordinary examples of individual courage, both of which won the Medal of Honour, the highest American military distinction. Without doubt the most popular recipient of this award was Second-Lieutenant Audie L. Murphy of the 15th infantry regiment (3rd division). Obeying his division's motto 'We're staying put' he jumped onto a burning tank-destroyer and used its machine-gun to repulse two companies of Germans supported by six tanks. Though wounded in the leg and under attack from three sides, Second-Lieutenant Murphy broke up the enemy attack and saved his company.[1]

Still more moving is the story of Rodger Young (148th infantry regiment). Despite the fact that his sight and hearing were seriously affected by an accident at college, he joined up and received rapid promotion in the Pacific. However, he asked

1 A popular hero, he became a star of Western films, and was killed at the controls of his private plane in 1972.

AMERICAN ARMY, AIRBORNE TROOPS

1. Parachutist with Red Indian haircut—2. Parachutist with Thompson sub-machine-gun. Both are wearing the American flag on their right arm to assist in recognition by friendly troops.

Arm badges: 3. 17th Airborne division—4. 11th Airborne division—5. 13th Airborne division—6. 9th Airborne division—7. 82nd Airborne division. The letters AA stand for 'All American', a relic from the 1917 New York Division which was made up of very recently naturalised Americans—8. 101st Airborne Division.

9. Special version of the M1 A1 carbine for parachutists. Parachute troops had folding butts for jumping and firing from the hip, which could be unfolded when firing from the shoulder.

AIRBORNE

3

AIRBORNE

4

11

AIRBORNE

5

AIRBORNE

6

AIRBORNE

8

1

2

AIRBORNE

AA

7

9

L.J.F. Fünchen

to be returned to the ranks lest his infirmities endanger the lives of his colleagues. His regiment was fighting on the island of New Georgia in the Solomons on 31 July 1943 when his company was cut off and in danger of being surrounded. Armed only with grenades, Rodger Young attacked singlehanded a Japanese machine-gun emplacement that had cut off his company's retreat. Even though his position had been spotted, and he was twice wounded, he continued to attack while his companions escaped and gave up his life as he destroyed the enemy position. A popular song records Rodger Young's sacrifice:

'On the island of New Georgia in the Solomons
Stands a simple wooden cross alone to tell
That beneath the silent coral of the Solomons
Sleeps a man, sleeps a man remembered well.'

Light Arms

RIFLES

Of the 16,112,566 men of all arms who served under the American flag it is estimated that only slightly more than 2,000,000 carried rifles. In spite of this relatively low figure, it should be noted that the rifleman still had a very special place in an increasingly sophisticated and efficient war machine.

At the outbreak of hostilities the American infantry was issued with two models of rifle: either the Springfield of 1903 and 1917, or the US Enfield, also known as the American Enfield and inaccurately referred to in Britain as the 1917 Springfield. These were First World War veterans, and both gave way to a more efficient weapon; the Garand 30 MI semi-automatic rifle.

The Garand

This rifle entered mass production in 1939, and was first used by the army in the Pacific. After training a soldier could fire eight rounds in

twenty seconds with the MI and, taking his time, could hit a target at 450 metres. Its maximum range was more than 3,000 metres. General MacArthur was an enthusiastic supporter from the start and later General Patton said that the Garand was the best weapon ever invented. With the same 7.62mm calibre as its predecessors the Garand could fire tracer, armour-piercing and incendiary ammunition as well.

The MI Carbine

Made by Winchester under the name of 30 calibre MI carbine, this 1941 semi-automatic model was designed to replace the Colt automatic worn by non-commissioned officers and troops in certain special units. Weighing only 5lbs the MI had a 15-round magazine and was very popular. There was also a model with a folding butt for parachutists, called the M1A1. Another model, the M2, had a 30-round magazine and could be used to fire single shots, as a semi-automatic, or for firing in bursts. Only 550,000 M2 were produced as against 5,000,000 MIs.

SUB-MACHINE-GUNS

Designed to have the fire-power of a machine-gun and the weight of a rifle, the most famous if not the most efficient sub-machine-guns were the 192 and 1928 model Thompson 45s (11.43mm).

The 1928 Thompson differed from its predecessor in having a Cutt compensator or muzzle-brake to counteract the kick when the gun was used in short bursts. The Thompson's high rate of fire – 600–700 rounds a minute – made it hard to hold steady. In 1942 a modified and simpler version came out, known as the Thompson MI, distin

AMERICAN ARMY, LIGHT ARMS I

1. 1917 US Enfield 30 rifle—2. Garand's MI 30 semi-automatic rifle—3. 7.62mm MI automatic carbine (1 rounds) made by Winchester—4. M2 automatic carbin (30 rounds)—5. M3 45 calibre (11.43mm) sub-machine-gun or M3 A1 1944 model with 9mm Parabellum ammunition—6. 1942 Thompson MI machine-gun, 45 calibre—7. 191 Browning 30 calibre (7.62mm) A2 automatic rifle, known a BAR for 'Browning Automatic Rifle'—8. 1917 Brownin A1 machine-gun (7.62mm)—9. Browning M2 50 calibr (12.7mm) machine-gun. More than 2 million were made

guished mainly by its rougher finish and the absence of a front pistol grip.

In spite of its qualities, the Thompson was too heavy, too expensive and too sophisticated, and for this reason the army turned to a new sub-machine-gun far simpler in design and largely made of pressed steel soldered together. This had a dramatic effect on unit costs, which fell from 55 to 18 dollars per gun. Known as the US M3 45 (11.43mm), it was ungainly and ugly but reliable, and could if necessary be converted to take 9mm Parabellum ammunition.

We should not move on without mentioning the Thompson's famous forerunner, the Reising, which was used by the illustrious Marines.

THE BAR

While the American army was well equipped with a multiplicity of automatic or semi-automatic weapons, there was really only one automatic rifle, the old but remarkable 1918 model Browning 30 (7.62mm) automatic rifle commonly referred to as the BAR. With its magazine for 20 rounds of conventional, armour-piercing, tracer or incendiary ammunition, this heavy automatic rifle was mainly used by small infantry companies as support with its rapid rate of fire – 500 rounds a minute – its accuracy up to 550 metres and its maximum range of 3,200 metres.

Towards the end of the war some crack units like the Marines and the Rangers were issued with new automatic rifles, the 1941 Johnson light machine-gun and the 1944 Johnson.

MACHINE-GUNS

By far the most popular machine-gun was the Browning 50 calibre M2 (12.7mm). Basically the infantry's main defensive weapon, it was enthusiastically adopted by all three services as a light anti-aircraft gun. The M2 was used as an auxiliary weapon by all armoured corps, and in its specialised forms was practically the navy's and air force's only rapid fire armament of its calibre. Certainly the devastating effect of its heavy shot, spat out at the rate of 450 rounds a minute to a range of well nigh 6,400 metres, made it a truly awesome weapon.

The American equivalent of the Vickers, the 1917 model Browning A1 could keep firing for long bursts thanks to its water-cooled sleeve. It fired 12.7mm rounds at a rate of 400 to 520 a minute and had a maximum range of 3,650 metres, but was little used, for a flood of M2s came to replace it.

MORTARS

The 60mm M2 was the most manageable and the most powerful of its category in the US army. Far superior in range and destructive power to its British and German 50mm counterparts, it could throw a 3-lb bomb more than 2,000 yards. It weighed so little (32lbs in its second version) that it could be used by just one man. In normal practice it could fire 18 rounds a minute, but a fast gunner could raise this to 30 or 35 rounds a minute.

The US 81mm M1

Weighing some 60lbs, this weapon could fire 18/3 6-lb bombs about 3,000 yards. The 81mm was outstanding on all fronts, particularly in the assault on the Seigfried line.

The 105mm heavy mortar

Nicknamed the 'Goon Gun' by GIs, this was one of the infantry's favourite weapons. The 105mm fired 22-lb bombs 4,000 yards in 60 seconds. Extraordinarily accurate at short range, the mortar could drop a bomb through the open turret of an enemy tank as easily as a basket-ball player scores a goal.

A NEW WEAPON: THE BAZOOKA

With the Munroe effect[1] first noticed in 1888 as their point of departure, American artillery chiefs perfected the most famous of their inventions: a rocket launcher. Some facetious soldier nicknamed it the bazooka after a bizarre musical instrument made of stove pipes that Bob Burns the American inventor and cartoonist had created.

This revolutionary weapon was first tested in 1941 by Lieutenant E. G. Uhl who, unnecessarily as it transpired, wore an asbestos suit for his protection. Later in the year it was quietly tested on a wider scale with the gunner protected only by an army-issue gas mask. In the end even this precaution proved unnecessary and, once the breach of the bazooka had been fitted with a flame deflector, it could be fired quite happily without face protection. When ready to fire the loader put the rocket in the back of the bazooka and wired it to a spring contact on two dry-cell batteries. He would then tap the gunner on the shoulder to tell him the bazooka was loaded, and retire while the gunner pulled the trigger and fired the rocket off in a sheet of flame.

The Germans copied the bazookas when they captured them in Russia.

Armoured Vehicles

After two abortive attempts to set up a tank force at Fort Meade, Maryland in 1928, and at Fort Eustis, Virginia in 1931, the embryo of the Iron Cavalry as it was commonly (and significantly) called was based at Fort Knox, Kentucky in 1933. In 1938 the 1st and 3rd cavalry regiments made up from a few scattered units were turned into the 7th motorised cavalry brigade under Brigadier General Daniel van Voothis. At the end of the same year the brigade came under the command of a promising young officer who had long been fascinated by the problem of getting this new concept to work. He was Adna R. Chaffee and at that time was just a Colonel. Promoted almost at once to Brigadier General, this 55 year old officer left such a mark that he may well be called the Father of the armoured crops, a force which came into being on 10 July 1940, and finally put paid to the old-fashioned, over-cautious attempts to apportion the tanks between cavalry and infantry units.

Now grouped under their own command, the tanks of this first corps made up two armoured divisions and a reserve battalion. At that time there were less than 500 armoured vehicles, and none of them could have held out for long against even the weakest enemy armour. It must be remembered that for twenty years a host of orders, counter-orders and procrastinations had complicated this type of vehicle development, a confusion that centred on the brilliant American engineer Walter Christie and his avant-garde theories.

AMERICAN ARMY, TANKS I

1. 1938 M2 A2 E3 light tank; a few fought in Burma—2. M A1 medium tank called 'General Lee' in Great Britain. This tank and the 'Grant' (fig. 3) were the backbone of the British army at the second battle of El Alamein in October 1942—3. 1942 M3 A5 medium tank, known as the 'General Grant' in the British Army, who had modified the turret. It was the first American medium tank to fight in Africa where, at the battle of Gazala in May 1942, it gave the Germans an unpleasant surprise. However, its great height made it an easy target for Rommel's 88s, though perhaps it did not deserve its nickname of 'ELH' (Egypt's Last Hope)—4. M3 A1 light tank called 'General Stuart' or Stuart Mark IV, nicknamed 'Honey' as a tribute to its performance. It was the first American light tank to enter combat at Sidi Rezegh in Libya in November 1941.

5. Arm badge of the 1st American armoured division, nicknamed 'Old Ironside', which was based at Fort Hood, Texas. It fought in Algeria and Tunisia, then at Salerno and Paestum in 1943, and at Anzio and Rome in 1944. The 2nd, 3rd and 4th armoured divisions had the same badge; only the number changed. The combination of the colours yellow, blue and red was intended to symbolise the union of the cavalry, infantry and artillery within the armoured corps.—6. The 65th cavalry division—7. The 62nd cavalry division—8. The original 1938 uniform (7th cavalry brigade) —9. Burma battledress with a 1928-model Thompson A (11.43mm).

1 See below for an explanation of the hollow charge in the chapter on artillery.

1

5

6

7

2

3

T·24889

4

8   9

F. Funcken

His first armoured vehicle dated back to 1919 and, despite a superficial resemblance to the French Renault tank, had many revolutionary features. Unfortunately the 1920 National Defence Act, which for financial reasons suppressed the Tank Corps, had created the least favourable climate imaginable for Christie's work. Undismayed, between 1921 and 1931 he kept suggesting a series of vehicles called combat cars (a formula to get round the 1920 law which forbade the use of tanks by cavalry regiments).

Christie's inventions were unique in that they prolonged track life by making a rapid conversion (in about 30 minutes) to road wheels possible for getting to the battle field. Thus equipped, the 1928 model could reach the astonishing speed of 75 mph, but when the terrain called for the use of tracks they proved inefficient. Refusing to be discouraged, Christie brought out a new model – the T3 – in 1931, also known as the T1 Combat Car in the cavalry. The army bought three and Russia, two. Ironically Russia was the only country fully to benefit from the dogged American's genius, as they went on to develop the Bystrokhodnii or BT series, today recognised as the forerunner of modern tanks.

They say that no prophet is honoured in his own country but it is still a frightening thought that Christie's genius was exploited only in a country whose ideology was diametrically opposed to his own. From then on Christie sank into the realms of science-fiction invention by trying to perfect a flying tank; an impossible dream that some still cherish today. The last of the Christie-inspired tanks was the T4 E1, later called the T4 medium tank.

As happened in other countries, the Ordnance Corps then made the mistake of opting for light tanks which were cheaper and more economical to run. In this way the M1 Combat Car was born and, when rigged out with two turrets for infantry, became the M2 A1, the US army's last infantry tank.

In 1940 there was an obvious need for a medium tank, and the M3 or 'General Lee' was selected, 5,000 being mass-produced from July 1941. It was supplied to Great Britain in large quantities through the Lend-Lease agreement[1] signed by the two countries in March 1941, and was the first American medium tank involved in actual fighting in Libya. More than 10ft high, this fortress on wheels had some initial success, but turned out to be a sitting duck for Rommel's 88mm guns.

An English version with a modified turret appeared at the end of 1942, called the M3 A5 or 'General Grant'. In spite of its shortcomings the M3 stayed in service until 1944, though it was only used in certain limited roles.

Work on the second medium tank, the M4, began in 1941 and full-scale production began in July 1942. Destined to be the most famous of American tanks, 42,234 M4s were built, more than any other and almost half the total of all tanks produced, which amounted to 88,410. Better

1 The Lend-Lease Act allowed the President of the United States to supply equipment to any country whose defence he considered of importance to the United States. This aid was unusual in that it was not necessarily given in exchange for money but for any help, however indirect, to the US, such as a stabilisation of the world balance of power. Some 40 billion dollars were expended by the Lend-Lease programme, with Great Britain (42%), the USSR (28%), China and free France as the principal beneficiaries.

AMERICAN ARMY, TANKS II

1. 1942 M5 Stuart light tank. Its stabilised gun meant that it could shoot accurately while on the move. A direct development of the M3 Stuart light tank, it took part in the Allied landings at Casablanca in North Africa in 1942. Used as a reconnaissance tank in Italy and France, it was employed in Normandy with a sawtooth device which cut grass.—2. 'General Sherman' M4 A4 medium tank (1942) here shown in the colours of the British 5th Lancers. It replaced the British army's 'Lees' and 'Grants'. After the 2nd battle of El Alamein, it became the most famous of all American tanks. Nearly 50,000 were built, more than the enemy could destroy.—3. M4 A3 E8 Sherman (1944), a final development of the former with a 76mm high velocity gun. Far superior to its predecessor, it outclassed the 'Panther'—4. 105mm US gun motor carriage self-propelled gun nicknamed the 'Priest' by the English because its turret looked like a pulpit. It appeared at El Alamein in 1943 with the 5th Royal Horse Artillery regiment. Not one of the 90 that took part in the battle was hit. The drawing shows a 'Priest' used by the Free French.

5. Tank crewman in 1944/45 winter dress (4th armoured division) with fur-lined jacket worn over one-piece combination with the latest lace-up boots. The gun is a 1942 Thompson M1 45 calibre (11.43mm)—6. American-type tank crew helmet.

1

2

3

5

6

4

F Funcken

known as the Sherman, this tank was immediately successful in North Africa, especially in the second battle of El Alamein, and large quantities were given to the Russians.

The M4 was simple and rugged, had a very mobile turret, bogey suspension, a V8 motor giving it a speed of 25 mph and first-rate tracks that lasted for 3,000 miles of road – five times longer than an equivalent German tank. At the end of the war the 'General Pershing' tank appeared, a combination of the Sherman medium and M6 heavy tanks, but it arrived in Europe too late to make any impression.

In the light tank category, the M5 'Stuart', a direct development of the M3 'Stuart' entered service during the allied invasion of North Africa in 1942. It accompanied the landings in Sicily, Italy and France because its height and weight meant that it could be carried on lightweight assault craft.

By 1944–1945 the two small armoured divisions of Major-General Chaffee (1884–1941) had become sixteen magnificent divisions which had fully proved their creator's theories.

SELF-PROPELLED GUNS

Pre-occupied with the need to supply her troops with armoured vehicles, America was somewhat slow in developing this particular category. The first self-propelled gun was the M6 Gun Motor Carriage with a 75mm gun. The most famous was the M7 with a 105mm howitzer that the British nicknamed the 'Priest'. Tank-destroyers were finally rendered obsolete by the growing number of tanks available, for a tank was the best means of destroying another tank. This was borne out after the war by the disbanding of the Tank Destroyer Command.

American Planes

In the previous chapters, the reader will have become aware of the great progress made by American industry in the war effort. And yet it

TABLE OF PRINCIPAL AMERICAN ARMOURED VEHICLES FROM 1941 TO 1945

TYPE	WEIGHT	SPEED	RANGE	ARMAMENT	CREW	USE
Light Tanks:						
M2 A2 E3	9.6 tons	48 km/h	370 km	1 12.7mm machine-gun 2 7.6mm machine-guns	4	Some in Burma
M3 A1 Stuart III	13 tons	59 km/h	135 km	1 37mm cannon 2 7.6mm machine-guns	4	1941 in Libya: 1st US tank involved in large-scale battle
M5 Stuart VI	15 tons	64 km/h	270 km	1 37mm cannon 3 7.6mm machine-guns	4	1942 in Casablanca
Medium Tanks:						
M4 A4 'General Sherman'	32.9 tons	40 km/h	193 km	1 75mm cannon 3 7.6mm machine-guns	5	More were built than the enemy could destroy

AMERICAN FIGHTER PLANES

1. North American P-51D 'Mustang', the best American fighter and the one built in the largest quantities, particularly of version D—2. North American P-51B 'Mustang'—3. Republic P-47 'Thunderbolt'. Although superseded as a high altitude escort by the 'Mustang' it had numerous successes. Major S. Gabreski, one of the great American aces in Europe, scored 31 kills with P-47s—4. Grumman 'Hellcat', the US Navy's best fighter—5. Curtiss P-40N, nicknamed the 'Kittyhawk' in Great Britain. The N version was the most common—6. Lockheed P-38 'Lightning' Although fewer of these were built than of the other fighters the P-38 was the highest scorer against the Japanese air force—7. Bell P-39 'Airacobra'—8. Curtiss P-40 'Warhawk'

Markings: 9. Until 1942—10. From 18 August 1942 until 30 June 1943. In North Africa this badge sometimes had a yellow border, British style.—11. From 30 June 1943 to September 1943—12. From September 1943 to 1947

was in airpower that this great nation showed its strength most clearly.

One of Roosevelt's advisers claimed that the notion of airpower destroying an enemy army was pure fantasy, so that a ludicrously small annual budget of only 74 million dollars was voted for the air force, and as a result, the US air force in 1939 was rated third or fourth only in the world. If at first American pilots had to fight in outmoded aircraft it was entirely the fault of this adviser, even though by 1940 the budget had been raised to 224 million dollars. At all events, the sum was increased in the following year by a factor of 17 to 3,708 million dollars, to rise the next year to the incredible sum of 22 thousand millions, and again in 1944 to a peak of 23,659,000,000 dollars. Such fabulous sums of money furnished the air force with 120,000 planes of all kinds in four years and, by the end of the war, with some 60,000 planes on the Pacific front alone.

With her fighters divided up into fifteen air forces and a Bomber Command of superfortresses, the Americans could pride themselves on having the most powerful air force in the world.

THE FIRST BATTLES

Disregarding the morality involved, the Japanese surprise attack on Pearl Harbour on 7 December 1941 was a model of its kind. 8 battleships, 8 cruisers and numerous other vessels were sunk or suffered damage. Of more particular concern here were the American air force's losses, and these were heavy: 141 fighters and bombers were destroyed and an even larger number damaged to some extent; 150 navy planes were destroyed or damaged before they could fire a shot. Of the 353 Japanese planes that took part in the massacre only 29 planes and 55 men were lost.

This baptism of fire would be long remembered by the air force. Imagine the pilots' feelings as they watched their Curtiss P-40s being destroyed on the ground, where they were drawn up in tight lines as if on parade, their fuel tanks empty and their guns not loaded for fear of sabotage. It can be readily understood that the first months after

the catastrophe of Pearl Harbour were a difficult time for the air force; yet still they managed to hold off Japanese attacks. The blindness of those who had underestimated the enemy cost many flyers their lives.

These mistakes were corrected so quickly that within the space of less than a year America began to take the initiative and enemy superiority in the air was on the decrease. From the spring of 1943 the air force could pride itself not only on having numerical superiority but also – and what was more important – on having far better planes technically.

FIGHTERS

At least until 1943, fighters in America were not considered as important as bombers and, as a result, they were markedly inferior to the enemy's planes.

The Bell P-39 'Airacobra' and the Curtiss P-40 'Warhawk' are good examples of this, and yet they represented half of the total air force, which makes their pilots' achievements all the more remarkable. A pilot became an ace when he had chalked up 5 confirmed enemy aircraft destroyed, so that some lucky pilots managed to become 'aces in a day'.

The three best long-range fighters involved in breaking the Luftwaffe's stubborn resistance were without doubt the twin-engined Lockheed P-38

AMERICAN BOMBER PLANES I

1. Martin B-26 'Marauder' — 2. Examples of group badges — 3. Consolidated B-24J 'Liberator' (British nickname). From September 1943 the red edging of the stars was replaced with dark blue — 4. Disposition of machine-gunners — 5. Examples of insignia — 6. North American B-25H 'Mitchell' — 7. Example of insignia — 8. Nose of a B-25J-type of the 'Air Apaches'; a version with an all-metal nose was built from 1943 onwards, to take extra machine-guns for ground attack duties. The planes were coloured according to their theatre of operations, but in some cases, as for instance in the raid on Ploesti, different kinds of camouflage were mixed together in the same bomber group: sand colour, brown and green, beige and olive all used together. There was even one Liberator in vivid orange flown by George Winger who was killed during a raid. With the end of the war the planes were left unpainted since the enemy were unlikely to attack them on the ground.

2

1

3

4

5

6

7

8

'Lightning', the Republic P-47 'Thunderbolt' and the North American P-51 'Mustang'.

The 'Lightning'

Although fewer (9,923) were made than other fighters, the 'Lightning' was one of the best at destroying German and Japanese planes. It was the first escort plane to appear on the European front and flew with the bombers that struck deep into Germany up to 1944, for it was able to deal with German fighter planes flying in their own airspace.

The Japanese for their part, though less easily impressed, said they feared and hated the 'Lightning' more than any other American fighter. Lieutenant Richard Bong flew a 'Lightning' to notch up his 40 victims in the Pacific, as did four of the ten highest scoring aces in the US air force.

The 'Thunderbolt'

Originally conceived as a light fighter, the 'Thunderbolt' in its final development was the largest and heaviest fighter the US had ever built.

It appeared in combat in 1943 and soon won a reputation as a tough and rugged machine. Quite often P-47s returned from missions with more holes than a sieve and, after minor repairs, took off again the next day.

In Italy 'Thunderbolt' pilots developed a special way of dealing with particularly tough emplacements located in mazes of ruined houses: diving on their target, they would drop their long-range tank still full of fuel, so that it burst open as it struck the rubble. Then, making another pass, they would fire incendiary bullets which set the fuel on fire. No blockhouse, however well buried, could stand up to this treatment.

The 'Mustang'

The 'Mustang' entered service in 1943 and was made in greater numbers than any other fighter. Though there were serious reservations when it was conceived, it was without doubt the best fighter that America produced, and the Senate Commission of Investigation concurred in this opinion. Some writers go so far as to say that it was

the best fighter of the Second World War.

The 'Mustang' flew its first missions in 1943 as escort for the RAF bombers, a job which made its reputation. The awesome efficiency of the P-51 can be seen from the fact that the 4th Group alone scored 1,016 enemy aircraft destroyed.

BOMBERS

One feat alone would ensure American bombers a place in history. On 18 April 1942 16 North American B-25 'Mitchells' under Lieutenant-Colonel J. H. Doolittle took off from the aircraft carrier *Hornet* for the legendary 30-second raid on Tokyo. The result was insignificant in material terms but had a profound effect on morale, since it shook the unquestioning self-confidence of the Japanese, and went some way towards satisfying America's thirst for revenge.

The Boeing B-17 'Flying Fortress' which flew with the RAF from 1941 can be seen as the embodiment of US airpower, so universally famous did it become.

At Pearl Harbour there had been 114 in service but by the end of the war there were more than 12,700. The later B-29 'Superfortress' began its spectacular raids on Japan in 1943, and it was a B-29 named the *Enola Gay* which dropped the first atom bomb on Hiroshima.

Almost as famous, but smaller in size, the B-2 Consolidated 'Liberator' flew extensively from 1941 to 1945. 'Go anywhere, do anything' might well have been the Liberator's watchword.

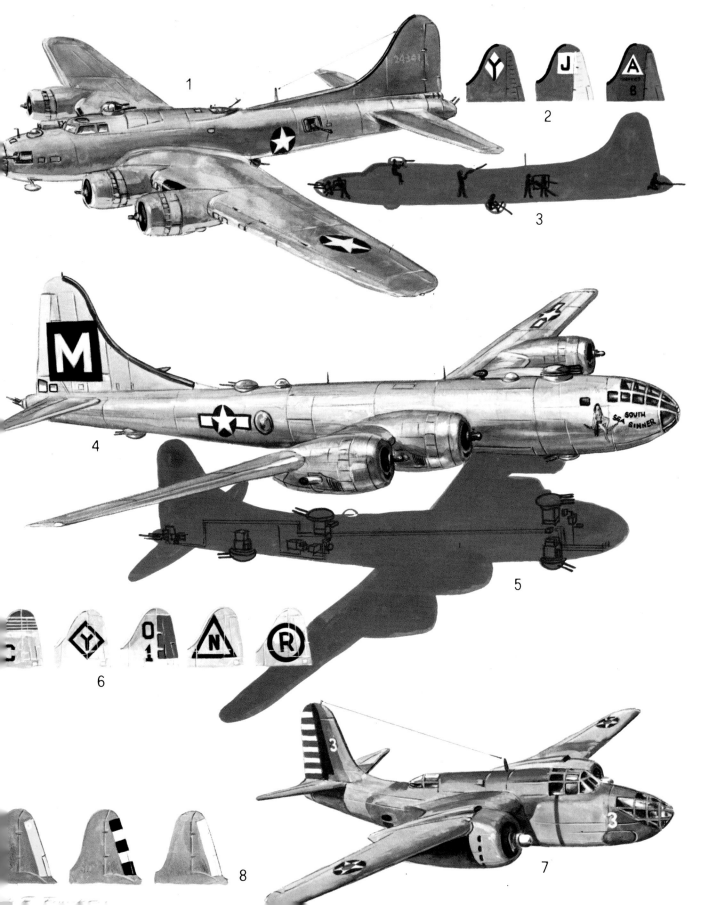

1

2

3

M

4

SOUTH SEA SINNER

5

6

7

8

The 'Liberator' served on all fronts and dropped a total of 635,000 tons of bombs that destroyed 4,189 enemy aircraft. 178 B-24s of the 9th Air Force flew in the famous raid against the Rumanian oil fields of Ploesti. 446 men were lost and, according to the official reports, 53 planes, although in fact only 33 'Liberators' returned in flying condition. The daylight raids on Germany without fighter escort from July to October 1943 resulted in such losses that they had to be given up pending the arrival in February 1944 of large numbers of long-range fighters.

From then on German cities were subjected to increasingly heavy raids. But, contrary to what one might think, it was not this terrible massacre of civilians which broke Germany's spirit; indeed, it only served to harden it. In fact it was the systematic destruction of her petroleum industry, and more especially of her lines of communication, that forced Germany to surrender.

JAPAN

The Sphere of Co-Prosperity

During the period of 1875–1899 Japan had embarked on her systematic progress of territorial expansion by seizing the Kuril and Bonin Islands, the Ryukyu Archipelago, the Pescadores Islands, the wealthy island of Formosa as well as Marcus and Volcano Islands. The dazzling victory against the Russians in 1910 won the whole Korean peninsula, and ten years later the victors of the First World War gave their allies the Marshall Islands, the Caroline Islands and the Marianne Islands. Under the mandate given them by the League of Nations the Japanese were not meant to build any kind of fortifications on these islands, but their cavalier treatment of this restriction enabled them to become the foremost naval power in the Pacific.

With rare determination, the Japanese pursued their colossal plan to make their nation the leader of Asia, by trying first to acquire the raw materials needed for heavy industry. In 1931 Manchuria was attacked, then China in 1937, and soon huge arsenals and depots, factories and synthetic petrol distilleries were being put into action.

Significantly, the war that had broken out in Europe in 1939 immobilised almost all the Allied troops in that area at the very time when important European interests were being threatened in the

JAPANESE ARMY I

1. 1930 M90 uniform—2. 1938 M98 uniform—3. M98 uniform and equipment—4. M90 uniform with M98 cap—5. Officer in M90 field service dress with rank insignia worn on the shoulders. The hilt of his own personal sword is covered with a canvas sheath to protect its decorated handle. No two swords were alike, even varying as to length. They were often several generations old and were true works of art—6. Officer in M98 field service dress with rank insignia on the collar—7. Soldier in a mortar team—8. Soldier with a 50mm model 98 mortar—9. Officer wearing gas mask—10. Soldier with 1911 model 44 cavalry carbine with folding bayonet.

Rank insignia: 11–13. General Officers: General, Lt-General, Major-General—14–16. Senior Officers: Colonel, Lt- Colonel, Major—17–19. Subalterns: Captain, First Lieutenant, Second-Lieutenant—20. Non-commissioned officers: Sergeant-Major. These badges were the same as those worn on the collar of the M98 (1938) uniform, but were in the form of elongated rectangles, worn across the shoulders on the 1930 M90 uniform. Epaulettes (second row) were worn with the 1938 model service dress. Stripes corresponding to the different ranks were worn on coats, macintoshes etc.

21. Officer's peaked cap—22. Cap insignia of the Imperial Guard—23. Officer's field service cap—24. A system of fastening with laces—25. Officer's peaked cap with canvas visor.

Far East. Germany's victories in the west, followed by her attack on Russia, only served to help Japan's imperialist expansion.

It has often been suggested that Japan declared war on the Allies in order to reach what she called the 'Sphere of Co-prosperity' at one stroke. But it seems rather that when they attacked the United States their strategy was based on the hope of a limited war. They believed it was necessary to destroy or neutralise American forces in the Pacific, and then to seize Malaysia, the Dutch East Indies, the Philippines, Guam, the Wake and Gilbert Islands, Thailand and Burma. Once this had been achieved, the Allies would be unable to break through these powerful defences and would have to settle for a negotiated peace.

After Pearl Harbour the Japanese achieved in a few weeks an advance which logically should have taken several decades, and which far surpasses the German *Blitzkriegs*. But these colossal victories were fatal for Japan, since they sparked off an immense explosion of indignation throughout America, which was to upset all the carefully prepared Japanese plans.

The Japanese Soldier

Japanese soldiers were famous for their fearlessness in the face of death. On compulsory call-up at the age of nineteen they were categorised according to physical condition: those in first class health were called A or B1; the short-sighted or hard of hearing, B2 or B3; while those relegated to class C went into the second army or third reserve.

With the coming of war and its increasing demands on manpower, the B2 and B3 classes who made up the first and second reserves were also called upon to fight, as were the nationals of previously conquered countries, such as Formosa and Korea.

While every soldier must accept the possibility of death, for the Japanese soldier death was something different. It was a matter of religion, for according to the Shinto creed, the Imperial family were Gods and all Japanese were descended alike from the Sun Goddess. Thus all Japanese considered themselves to be of one family, and more, as a race apart, superior to the rest of mankind because of their divine origin. Such holy respect for the family, inculcated from earliest youth, implied total obedience to parents, and through them, to the Emperor, who could ask anything of his subjects, even senseless death.

JAPANESE ARMY II

1. Cavalry Officer (green insignia above the pocket) in service dress—2. Officer in greatcoat—3. Officer in hooded cape—4. Officer in tropical dress (see note on swords on preceding page)—5. General Officer in full dress—6. Soldier of Landing Assault Troops with 1929 model 89 50mm grenade launcher—7. Sniper in jungle camouflage with 1937 model 97 6.5mm sniper rifle—8. With gas mask—9. Trooper with 1911 model 44 6.5mm carbine. The fur-lined sleeveless jacket was replaced by a padded waistcoat worn under the tunic—10. Soldier with cap and model 90 greatcoat. The model 98 greatcoat had only one row of buttons.

11. Acting Officer—12. Acting Officer in the reserves—13. Sergeant-Major—14. Sergeant—15. Corporal. The second row of epaulettes was worn with the 1938 service dress. The sleeves of winter and rain-clothes bore a strip (third row). The lower row shows the equivalent badge of rank as worn on tropical uniforms.—16. Corporal 2nd Class—17. Senior soldier. With the red and yellow chevron he is awaiting promotion to Corporal. Even so this badge was only worn on the shirt or hat.—18. Senior soldier with below, the red chevron worn with all traditional uniforms.—19. Private 1st Class awaiting promotion to senior soldier—20. Private 1st Class—21. Private 2nd Class

22. Model 90 (1930) collar tabs—23. Soldier's field service cap—24. Service peaked cap—25. New style insignia worn after 1940. Colour indicates the arm:
yellow: artillery
red: infantry and tanks
black: military police
garnet: engineers
medium green: cavalry
sky blue: air force
medium blue: transport
lilac: administration
dark green: health service
dark blue: veterinary
white: military justice
gold: music.
With the old model 90 uniforms, different arms were shown by the colour of the collar tab (fig. 22).

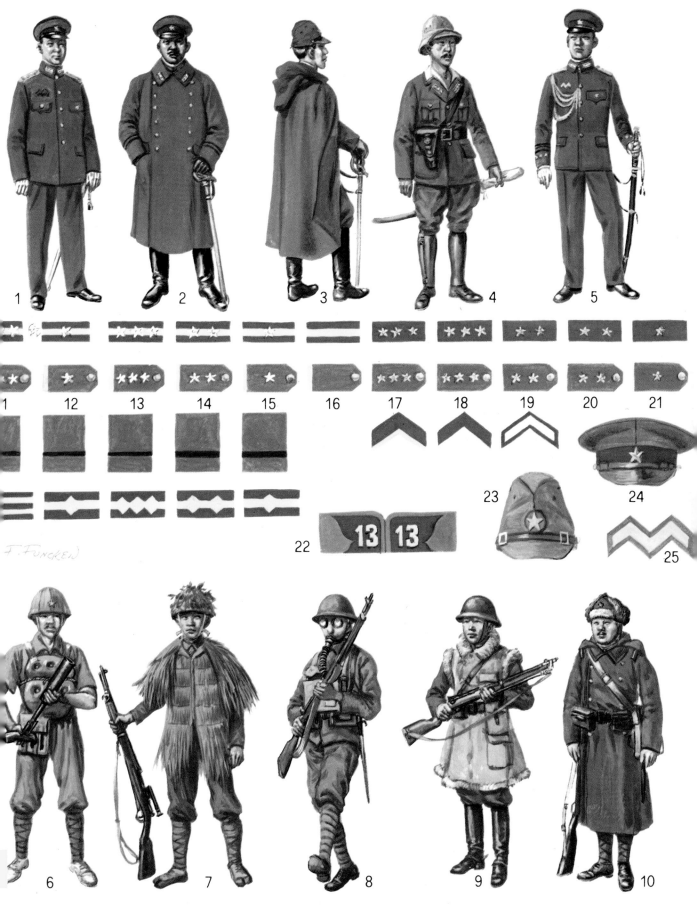

This servitude was upheld and developed in the army with a series of 'spiritual training sessions' or *Seishinkyoitu* to impart both a spiritual education and a fighting spirit. The old martial art of *bushido* with its Buddhist leanings made them regard sacrifice as a matter of honour, courage and purity. Absolutely secure in the belief of their superiority over other men, Japanese soldiers were convinced that they were fulfilling a sacred duty in the subjugation of humanity for its eventual good.

Throughout the war, their soldiers had the reputation of continuing to fight desperately even when all was lost, and this spirit was reinforced by the loss of face involved in being taken prisoner; indeed so powerful was this sense of shame that some soldiers have stayed in the jungle to this day rather than return home defeated.

To an ideology so disconcerting to the westerner one should add an extremely rugged military training, in the form of forced marches, living rough in all climates, and the very sophisticated use of camouflage. Paradoxically, though they excelled in the use of other weapons. Japanese soldiers – even snipers and sharpshooters – were only average marksmen with the rifle.

UNIFORMS

In addition to traditional or special-purpose uniforms, two distinct types were worn together. The model 90 (after the year 2590 by the Japanese calendar, or 1930 by ours) was by far the most common and was never completely replaced by the later model 98 of 1938.

The mustard-coloured model 90 was absolutely identical to the uniform worn in the 1914–1918 war, with the same swallow-tail tabs on a high collar.[1]

Different services were distinguished by the colour of their collar tabs:

black	military police	light green	cavalry
bright red	infantry & tanks	lilac	commissariat
yellow	artillery	dark green	medical
garnet red	engineers	violet	veterinary
dark blue	transport	gold	music
sky blue	air force	white	justice

These same colours were used on the second uniform, the model 98, but in the form of a splayed-out 'M' worn on the tunic above the right breast pocket. The main characteristic of the model 98 was the way the collar folded over so that it could be worn open in warm weather. The fabric was of a slightly lighter colour – khaki or olive green. Both uniforms had cotton versions for the hot season.

Officers

The principal uniforms of the officers are shown in the illustrations, but it should be noted that they were not provided by the State and that as a result there were many minor variations of cut and colour, ranging from khaki to the darkest olive-green.

The Ranks

Depending on whether the model 90 or model 98 was worn, the oblong rectangles identifying the wearer's rank were placed a) on the model 90 – one above the other on the shoulder; b) on the model 98 – one on each side of the collar, and rather smaller in size (18mm × 40mm). The illustrations show the positioning of insignia on other uniforms.

Headgear

Combat officers and other ranks had a special light cap which could be worn under a steel helmet. It should be noted that an older type of helmet decorated with a star flush-soldered on top and with a neck shield, was still in use. Neither afforded

1 See vol. 1 of *Arms and Uniforms of the First World War*.

JAPANESE ARMY III

1. Senior private (NCO candidate) with breast plate and model 96 (1936) 6.5mm automatic rifle—2. Infantryman with camouflaged helmet and jacket armed with model 10 (1940) 8mm sub-machine-gun—3. Naval infantryman with 6.5mm model 11 (1922) automatic rifle—4. Officer in the naval infantry—5. Sniper covered with special armour for fighting on the beach; he is shooting a 7.7mm model 9 (1939) rifle mounted on a bipod for greater accuracy—6.81mm model 99 mortar—7.90mm mortar—8. 1932 model 92 7.7mm calibre heavy machine-gun. Ammunition was in a fixed magazine attached horizontally on the left and is not visible here.

very effective protection. A rather complicated system of tapes very like that used on Samurai helmets kept this helmet in place. In summer helmet and cap could be worn with a neck-shield made up of four pieces of canvas. The flat cap was usually worn with service and ceremonial dress, except, to judge from photographs, in the case of some officers.

Light Arms

With its emphasis on infantry, the Japanese army had a wide range of light arms. There were three kinds of pistol, the 14, 26 and 94, all 8mm, and at least 12 kinds of rifle, not to mention quantities of weapons from at least fifteen enemy or allied countries.

SUB-MACHINE-GUNS

The only sub-machine-gun made in Japan was the 1940 model 100. Very expensive, it was to a great extent replaced by two imported German models, the Bergmann and the Solothurn.

BREN-GUNS AND MACHINE-GUNS

There were 3 types of bren-gun made between 1922 and 1939, and 5 types of machine-guns, of 6.5mm, 7.7mm and 13.2mm calibre.

MORTARS

This rugged and easily handled weapon was one of the Japanese army's most successful. In the 50mm range, captured 1912 model Chinese mortars were very similar to the purely Japanese 50mm model 10 (1921) and model 89 (1929), but these last had a hollow base which prompted the Americans to give them their nickname of 'Knee Mortars': anyone tempted to try firing them from

the knee could guarantee himself a broken femur

The next model, the 98 (1938), was of the same calibre but had a conventional base plate, and fired a strange box-shaped stick bomb. Later model had various calibres, 70mm, 81mm, 90mm 150mm and 250 mm, all similar to those of other nations.

Two simplified versions of the 70mm and 81mm mortars used a spike instead of a base plate. Simple to aim, they were used against low flying aircraft a technique never tried anywhere else as far a we know.

Armoured Vehicles

The Japanese did not build a tank (sensha) of their own before 1925. Up to that time the Mikado' armoured corps were equipped with medium and heavy British vehicles and a few little Renault FTs. Between the two wars Japanese engineer had time to study the tanks in action that the major powers built and began work on their own of which the first appeared in 1927. It weighed some 20 tons and carried an extra machine-gun in the rear.

The second model was the medium tank (ch sensha) model 89 (Japanese year 2589, our 1929 The M89, based on the Vickers C type wa followed in 1930 by a modified version of the 192

JAPANESE ARMOURED VEHICLES I

1. Tankette (sokosha) type 97 Teke light tank—2. Kei sensh type 93 light tank—3. Hago type 95—4. Chu sensha type 9 medium tank.

5. Naval colours with a 16-rayed sun. Tanks serving with th land forces either bore the star, or the national flag on a whi ground (figs 1 & 3), while tanks belonging to the nav infantry bore the naval colours or an anchor on the sta or both together—6. Tank insignia worn with general issu khaki uniform—7. Tank crew helmet. It seems that th Japanese standardised helmets and field service caps l making the size adjustable by a system of laces—8. Battl dress

1

2

3

5

6

7

8

4

R.F. Funcken

TABLE OF PRINCIPAL JAPANESE ARMOURED VEHICLES USED FROM 1939 TO 1945

TYPE	WEIGHT	SPEED	RANGE	ARMAMENT	CREW	USE
Bren-gun Carriers (*sokosha*) type 92	3 tons	40 km/h	160 km	1 7.7mm machine gun or 1 6.5mm machine-gun	2	In China from 1934
type 94	3.45 tons	40 km/h	200 km	1 7.7mm machine-gun	2	In China from 1934
type 97 'Teke'	4.9 tons	40 km/h	250 km	1 37mm cannon 1 7.7mm machine-gun	2	In 1937 with the motorised cavalry
Light Tanks (*kei sensha*) type 93	7 tons	40 km/h	250 km	1 13.2mm machin-gun 1 7.7mm machine-gun	3	1933
type 95	7.4 tons	40 km/h	250 km	1 37mm cannon 2 7.7mm machine-guns	3	Mass production began 1935
type 98	7.2 tons	50 km/h	300 km	1 37mm cannon 2 7.7mm machine-guns	3	1938
Medium tanks (*chu sensha*) type 89a	12.7 tons	25 km/h	140 km	1 57mm cannon 2 7.7mm machine-guns	4	1929; the oldest model used
type 89b	13 tons	25 km/h	170 km	1 57mm cannon 2 7.7mm machine-guns	4	1929; improvement of the former
type 95	14 tons	45 km/h	160 km	1 57mm cannon 2 7.7mm machine-guns	5	1935
type 97 'Chi-ha'	15 tons	38 km/h	210 km	1 47mm cannon 2 7.7mm machine-guns	4	1937; the best Japanese tank
type 97 'Shinhoto' (new turret) 'Chi-ha'	15.8 tons	38 km/h	210 km	1 47mm cannon 2 7.7mm machine-guns	4	1942; modified version of the former

model, called the model 91, whose only difference was thicker armour and an increase in weight of some 6 tons. Another heavy tank, very similar, the model 95 came out in 1935, as did numerous small tanks similar to western bren-gun carriers, named the Sokosha models 92, 94 and 97, the latter representing a considerable improvement.

The model 93 was the first light tank or *kei sensha* and then, following a modified version of this, came the Model 95 which was made in considerable numbers from 1935 to 1942.

Meanwhile the Japanese armoured forces grew from three regiments in 1933 to four the following year. This fourth regiment was the first tank brigade with a regiment of motorised infantry, artillery and pioneer corps. In 1939 the Japanese built more than 2,000 tanks. The Manchurian campaign of 1938–39 swelled the complement to two and then three armoured divisions, while each infantry division had two companies of light tanks. Although clearly inspired by the German armoured columns of the *Blitzkrieg*, the Japanese equivalent only took part in one lightning campaign in Malaysia and the Philippines. Everywhere else their armoured divisions were only used in small numbers and consequently played a minor and somewhat insignificant role.

The manufacture of armoured vehicles reached its peak in 1942 with a total of some 1,300 tanks to fall in 1944 to 295, and in 1945 to 130 tanks.

JAPANESE ARMOURED VEHICLES II

1. Type 97 medium tank (1942), with the anchor and naval colours—2. Naval model armoured car (1932)—3. 150mm self-propelled gun—4. Amphibious tank (1942)

1

2

3

L. & F. Funcken

4

The Japanese Air Force

The Japanese air force dates from 1909, so that when the First World War broke out only five years later the fledgling air force was quite incapable of playing any significant part. From 1911, however, the Japanese High Command set up two distinct air corps, one attached to the army and the other to the Imperial navy. The first squadrons were created with the help of French military advisers, and the first flying school opened its doors in 1920, to be followed two years later by two similar establishments.

The Great Powers showed little interest in these slow beginnings as they looked on disdainfully when the first models built under European or American licence emerged from the Japanese factories.

By 1935, after thirteen years of steady growth, the air force had eight 'flying regiments' or *hiko rentai*, a name which was changed to the apparently more war-like title of *hiko sentai*. At the same time the War Ministry took over production of war planes and more and more 'regiments' were created. As they grew more numerous these regiments were formed first into groups, then into brigades in 1940 which became aerial divisions in 1942, and, later still, developed into five air forces.

By this time the Japanese air force no longer raised a smile, for since the first weeks of the war in the Pacific it had achieved devastating successes. Japanese designers and engineers had been seriously underestimated: they had produced planes that were far more modern and original than expected. Furthermore, Japanese aircrew were quite as good as their machines, and for the most part had had active combat experience in the recent Russian and Chinese wars.

The most outstanding quality that Japanese fighter planes possessed was their remarkable manoeuvrability, achieved by sacrificing speed, armour-plating and heavy firepower. No doubt their pilots hoped that skill and courage would compensate for these handicaps, which was indeed the case until new American planes appeared. Then the losses were so great that Japanese in-dustry decided to switch to less manoeuvrable but better armed, better protected and faster planes, which were often comparable to the best planes the enemy flew.

The name of the best known Japanese fighter, the Zero, or model O, is indicative of the system used to name planes, tanks and weapons according to the year they appeared. O is for the year 2600 of the Japanese calendar (our 1940). Such simplicity is deceptive, and has caused considerable doubt and confusion in all areas. In aviation complications arose with different names for army and navy models of the same plane. The Americans evolved a simple code to avoid mistakes. Fighters were given a male Christian name such as Zeke, Paul or Claud; bombers, sea-planes and land based reconnaissance planes were called by female Christian names such as Betty, Dinah or Peggy, and transport planes took on names beginning with 'T'.

The catastrophic losses of 1944[1] led the Japanese air force to the desperate solution of suicide planes. Many different types of plane were used as *kamikaze* (meaning 'holy wind' after the hurricane which saved Japan from invasion in the thirteenth century). Those kamikaze pilots who flew the Ohkas belonged to a special corps called the *Jinrai Butai* or 'Holy Thunder' Corps. It is thought that about 2,600 pilots committed voluntary suicide in this way, and they were responsible for 50 per cent of the US navy's losses during the whole of the war.

1 7,800 planes and 12,000 aircrew were lost in the battle of Okinawa alone.

CHINA

First propounded by the Japanese in the *Tanaka Memorial* of 1927, the planned invasion of China began in 1931 with the capture of Manchuria, rich in iron and steel.

Hostilities recommenced on 7 July 1937 near Peking after a minor incident on the Marco Polo bridge had given the Mikado's troops the excuse they needed. The 300,000 strong Japanese army, reinforced with 150,000 Manchurians and Mongols, quickly occupied Peking and Tientsin, and then plunged into Mongolia while a part of the army was deployed in the Shanghai area. These troops were to invade Central China, to proceed up the Yangtze-Kiang and take Nanking, the National Chinese capital, and make contact with the troops who would by then have traversed Mongolia. This manoeuvre was designed to cut China in two and encircle most of Generalissimo Chiang Kai-shek's army. Nanking fell in December and was the scene of the most appalling atrocities the civilised world has ever seen.

The Japanese occupied the whole of Northern China as well as the greater part of Mongolia, but in spite of this defeat Chiang Kai-shek and the Communist General Chu Teh had succeeded in keeping their armies intact. The following year with Chinese resistance becoming increasingly stubborn Japan suffered the first defeat in her history, and lost 20,000 men in the battle of Taichung. Though the Japanese advance was not halted, it was forced to slow up, and finally came to a standstill when the dykes of the Yellow River were deliberately opened in an attempt to paralyse the Japanese army.

But still the Japanese held out, and eventually succeeded in taking all the major Chinese ports and industrial centres without, however, managing totally to quell resistance from Chinese troops and guerrillas. After four and a half years of floundering in China, Japan turned to other fields of conquest – Pearl Harbour, Malaysia and the Dutch East Indies.

The war with China continued, but now Chiang Kai-shek's army and Mao Tse-tung's Communist irregulars were getting help from America and the Soviet Union, and this was was to divert a million Japanese soldiers from the Pacific Islands where their eventual defeat was being prepared.

JAPANESE ARMY, AVIATION (pages 108–109)

1. Mitsubishi Zero-Zen (Zeke), the most famous Japanese fighter plane from 1941 to 1945—2. Mitsubishi A5 M4 (Claude). Naval fighter at the beginning of the war, it was relegated to the second line in 1942—3. Kawinishi N1 K2-J *Shiden-kai* – Purple Lightning (George 21), one of the navy's best fighters.—4. Mitsubishi Ki-21 (Sally), the standard bomber at the time of Pearl Harbour—5. Mitsubishi G3M (Nell), the navy's main bomber from 1941 to 1945. It was one of these planes that sank the *Prince of Wales* and the *Repulse*—6. Mitsubishi G4M (Betty), one of the most famous bombers from 1941 to 1945. With slight modifications it could carry an Ohka suicide plane to the vicinity of its target—7. Nakajima *Hayabusa* – Peregrine Falcon (Oscar). More fighters of this kind were built than any other—8. Mitsubishi Ki-67 *Hiryu* – Flying Dragon (Peggy). This replaced the Sally during the last year of the war—9. Nakajima *Hayate* – Hurricane (Frank). During the last year of the war, one of the most formidable planes the Allies had to face—10. Kawasaki Ki-61 *Hien* – Swallow (Tony), the army air force's best fighter. It appeared in March 1945—11. Mitsubishi Ki-46 (Dinah) a reconnaissance plane—12. Yokosuka MXY-7 *Ohka* – Cherry Blossom, nicknamed *Baka* ('crazy' in Japanese) by the Allies. Another special attack plane, but propeller driven, the Nakajima Ki-115 *Tsurugi* – Sword, was specially constructed as a suicide plane. About 100 were built but not in time to be used before the end of hostilities.

The Christian names in brackets following the planes' names above are part of the American-devised code used to identify them. The illustrations show the main type of paintwork used. Wings (*sentai*) were sub-divided into squadrons (*chutai*) which carried a badge on their tail: white for the first squadron, yellow for the second and red for the third. Although this was the general rule, there were without doubt numerous exceptions.

Chinese Uniforms

The first uniform dates from 1901 after the famous Boxer rising.[1] Dark blue at first, it changed to green-grey after the First World War, and by the time of the Sino-Japanese war it had become quite similar to the uniform worn by the enemy. The peaked cap, with a flat peak in the North, was of the ski-cap pattern in the South, and it was this southern model that became most commonly used.

In winter the whole uniform was lined, which gave the arms and legs a characteristically podgy appearance. In summer and when it rained a round straw hat was worn, some 60cm in diameter and rising to a point.

Mao Tse-tung's huge army of reserves did not wear uniforms.

Government and Communist troops alike used a bewildering cross-section of weapons from all over the world.

1 See *Arms and Uniforms 2 – 18th Century to the Present Day.*

CHINESE ARMY

Ranks of army: 1. General—2. Lieutenant-General—3. Major-General—4. Colonel (infantry)—5. Lieutenant-Colonel (justice)—6. Major (health service)—7. Captain (commissariat)—8. Lieutenant (army service corps)—9. Second Lieutenant and Adjutant (artillery)—10. Sergeant (infantry)—11. Lance-Sergeant (cavalry)—12. Corporal (artillery)—13. Lance-Corporal (engineers)—14. Private (commissariat)—15. Private 3rd class (health service)

Navy: 16. Admiral—17. Vice-Admiral—18. Rear-Admiral—19. Commodore—20. Captain—21. Commander—22. Lieutenant-Commander—23. Lieutenant—24. Sub-Lieutenant—25. Ensign. Note the subtly Chinese interpretation of the loop on the upper braiding worn by most ranks in the navy.

Air Force: 26. General—27. Lieutenant-General—28. Major-General—29. Colonel—30. Lieutenant-Colonel—31. Major—32. Captain—33. Lieutenant—34. Sub-Lieutenant

35. Insignia of the Nationalist Forces—36. Officer in service dress—37. Air force Officer—38. Naval Officer—39. Soldier in summer field service dress—40. Soldier in padded winter field service dress—41. Uniform of the Northern Army at the outbreak of hostilities—42. Revolutionary fighter under Mao Tse-tung.

43. The cruiser *Ping Hai*. Apart from 2 cruisers and 2 small destroyers, the Chinese fleet was made up mostly of small boats such as sloops and gunboats with an additional large number of river craft.

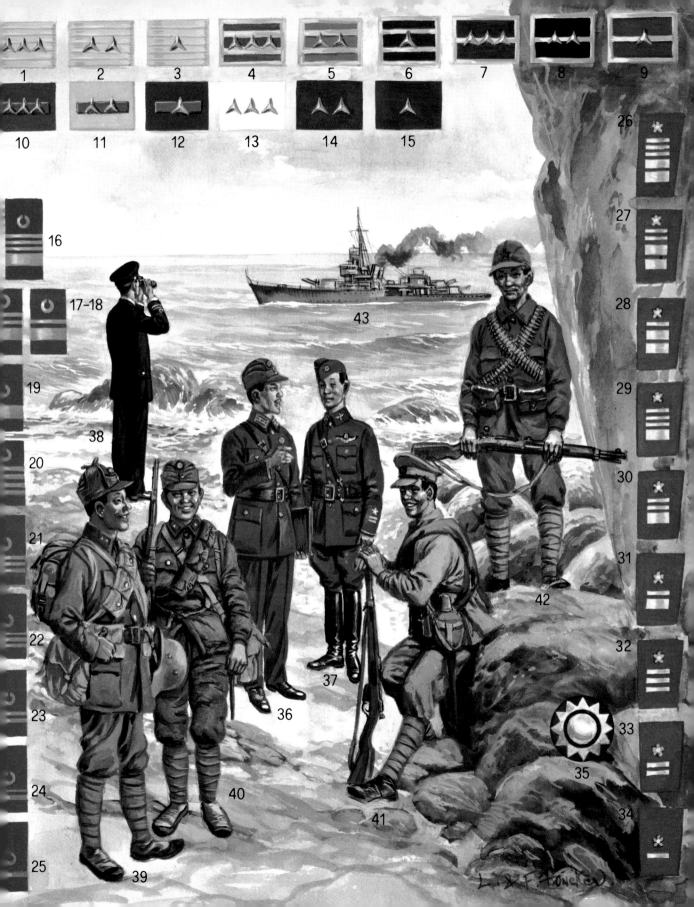